THE FRONTENAC LIBRARY
GENERAL EDITOR—GEOFFREY MILBURN
Althouse College of Education
University of Western Ontario

   Other titles in preparation

Conscription
in the Second World War
1939-1945

A STUDY IN POLITICAL MANAGEMENT

J. L. Granatstein

TORONTO
THE RYERSON PRESS

SBN 7700 0249 8

Acknowledgments
Where necessary, permission to quote
copyrighted material has been sought
through the publishers noted in the
relevant places.

The illustrations in this book have
been obtained from the following sources:
Public Archives of Canada, pp. 14, 56, 60, 69
The Toronto Star Syndicate, pp. 22, 25, 39
Microfilm Recording Co. Ltd., pp. 46, 62, 72
Toronto Public Libraries, p. 44

The publisher wishes to acknowledge with
gratitude those who have given their
permission to use copyrighted material in
this book. Every effort has been made to
credit all sources correctly. The author and
publisher will welcome information that will
allow them to correct any errors or omissions.

PRINTED AND BOUND IN CANADA
BY THE RYERSON PRESS, TORONTO

For Carole

Foreword

Although it is not the first series to take the whole field of
Canadian history as its subject, *The Frontenac Library* is
unique in its design and purpose. To counter oft-repeated, if
ill-founded, charges that Canadian history is dull or bland, the
books in the *Library* present the findings of scholars, not as
established truths, but as well considered opinions designed to
promote a reflective search for understanding. While discussing
a particular topic or problem, each author refers to, or quotes
from, important original sources, which are the raw materials
of the historian's craft. At the same time, where other interpretations exist, they are considered, not necessarily as opposing
theories, but as significant contributions to the dimensions of
an issue. Wherever possible, the questions, methods and pro-
cedures developed by sister disciplines in the humanities and
social sciences are used to adjust a focus too often predetermined
in the past by the constitutional viewpoint. In a very real sense,
therefore, we look over the shoulder of the historian and watch
him handle evidence or make judgments as he goes about that
creative task of writing which is the mark of his trade. Each
volume in the series is to be regarded as a responsible contribution to debate, an invitation to thought, and an opportunity
for personal assessment by the student.

    J. L. Granatstein's story of the conscription crisis in the
Second World War reveals deep divisions within the nation.
Many Canadians were unalterably opposed to enforced recruit-
ment as a means of obtaining manpower for armies overseas.
Yet, additional responsibilities assumed by Canada as part of the
allied war effort tended to persuade others that conscription
was both necessary and fair. At such a time, citizens were more
than usually sensitive to actions taken by their representatives

in government, and, always, the memory of a similar crisis in an earlier war worried the public—and haunted politicians. *Conscription in the Second World War* offers material for a classic study of decision making in a democracy.

The topic has further attractions for historians. Recent history is notoriously difficult to handle; where human emotions are strong, conclusions may be based on passionate conviction rather than on rational inquiry. Difficulties in criticizing surviving documents and in weighing earlier comments test historical skills. As an example of historical writing, and as an assessment of a very contentious issue, Dr. Granatstein's volume is doubly welcome. Furthermore, the drama of his subject is matched by his crisp and purposeful narrative.

G.M.

Preface

Conscription has been one of the most contentious issues in Canadian political history. On two occasions the issue disrupted relations between English and French Canadians and shook the political structure of the country. Both times, the questions involved were political ones more than military ones, although this did not always seem to be the case.

The key political question in 1917 and in 1942-44 was clearly whether or not national unity could be preserved. In 1917 it was not, and French Canada found itself virtually unrepresented in the seats of power in Ottawa. In the Second World War, however, the political gifts and compromising skills of Prime Minister Mackenzie King, a politician of extraordinary receptivity to the moods of Quebec, held the fabric of national unity together. This was a task of enormous difficulty. An analysis of how King achieved it forms the core of this book.

J. L. G.

Contents

TIME CHART

German troops invade Poland	September 1, 1939	
Britain declares war on Germany	September 3, 1939	
	September 10, 1939	Canada declares war on Germany
	October 25, 1939	Duplessis defeated in Quebec election by Liberals
	March 26, 1940	Federal Liberals sweep to victory in election
German invasion of France and Low Countries begins	May 10, 1940	
	May 13, 1940	R. J. Manion ousted as Conservative leader and replaced by R. B. Hanson
	June 21, 1940	*National Resources Mobilization Act* passed into law
Battle of Britain	Aug.-Sept., 1940	
	November 8, 1941	Arthur Meighen selected leader of Conservative party
Japanese attack Pearl Harbor	December 7, 1941	
Hong Kong garrison surrenders	December 25, 1941	
	January 22, 1942	King announces conscription plebiscite
	February 9, 1942	Meighen defeated in York South by-election
	April 27, 1942	Conscription plebiscite— Quebec votes "No" and English Canada "Yes"
Canadians in abortive Dieppe raid	August 19, 1942	
	December 11, 1942	Conservatives choose John Bracken as leader
D Day: Normandy invasion	June 6, 1944	
	Oct.-Nov., 1944	Conscription crisis in King cabinet
	June 11, 1945	Liberals win federal election with reduced majority

Chapter I

The Great War and After: 1914-39

The beginning of the Great War was welcomed with obvious enthusiasm in Canada. Everyone believed that the war would be short and glorious, full of dashing cavalry charges, chivalry, and adventure. There might be a few casualties, of course, but no one seriously believed that the war would last more than a few months. The world economic structure could not stand the strain, or so the learned professors advised.

The rush to the colours in Canada was remarkable. Men from all walks of life competed for a place in one of the regiments lucky enough to be ordered to report to Valcartier, Quebec. Sam Hughes, the Minister of Militia and Defence, had ordered an immense camp constructed there to receive the contingent. Wealthy men donated machine guns or trucks, and the Minister was besieged with requests for positions in the force. No one expected the war to be going on when the Canadians arrived overseas, but the ocean voyage was sure to be great fun. Canadians had met the first call.

Or had they? In fact, of the 36,267 men of the first contingent, only 10,880 were born in Canada. The great bulk of the remainder, more than 23,000, was born in the British Isles. Seen in this light, the casual references to enthusiasm in Canada appear rather strange. Canadians were enthusiastic, but not so enthusiastic as to rush off and enlist. The great majority of Canadian-born in the first contingent were members of the militia, people with a clear interest in the military life. The man on the street may have come out to cheer the departing soldiers, but it was business as usual for the stay-at-homes.

Professor Arthur Lower in his book, *Canadians in the Making*, sees this Canadian response as being significant. The deeper a man's roots in Canada, he says, the less likely he was

1

to volunteer to go and fight a strange war in a foreign land. The western provinces, where men still had shallow roots, furnished a disproportionately large share of men to the first contingent. Country dwellers were less involved than city people. And, as it turned out, French Canadians were less involved than English Canadians.[1]

FRENCH CANADA VIEWS THE WAR

French Canada's response was to be the cause of the great tragedy of war-time Canada. French Canadians simply did not share the enthusiasm that their English-speaking countrymen developed for "Britain's" war. In August, 1914 crowds had cheered in the streets of Montreal and sung the "Marseillaise", but this emotional binge petered out quickly. It was replaced with a sullen response, a shrugged comment that it was not Canada's war, that Canada owed nothing to England and less to France.

Hugh McLennan, the author of a novel on the Canadian dilemma entitled *Two Solitudes*, has one of his characters expound on the attitude of the *Québecois*:

> He thought of the war and the English with the same bitterness. How could French-Canadians — the only real Canadians — feel loyalty to a people who had conquered and humiliated them, and were Protestant anyway? France herself was no better; she had deserted her Canadians a century and a half ago, had left them in the snow and ice along the Saint Lawrence surrounded by their enemies, had later murdered her anointed king and then turned atheist . . . if a people deserted God they were punished for it, and France was being punished now.[2]

Quebeckers had no love for either England or France; nor were they entirely happy with the way they were being treated within Confederation. To Quebec Confederation had not been a coming together of provinces. Rather, it was supposed to have been a breaking apart of the strait-jacketed Union of the Canadas, a freeing of the provinces so that it could control its own destiny in areas that it believed to be important. To French

Canadians, Canada was a country of two peoples, each with equal rights.

English Canadians had violated this compact, or so the French province believed. The west had been seized by the English of Ontario, and Louis Riel, who was clearly insane, had been hanged by the vengeful federal government at Ottawa. Manitoba had tried to destroy the Roman Catholic religion and the French language in its schools and had come very close to success. And for what reasons? In French-Canadian eyes, these acts had been the product of Anglo-Saxon presumptions of racial superiority. The English-speaking, it was said, viewed the French as a weak minority of inferior status, as second class citizens. The same people who had demanded that Canada send troops to crush the Boers of South Africa in 1899 were running amok in Canada itself and French Canadians felt threatened.

More recently, action had been taken to limit the teaching of French in Ontario schools. Regulation 17 of the Ontario Department of Education was the culprit here. On every front, French Canadians saw themselves being pushed tighter and tighter into their own province. Whether these French-Canadian attitudes were based on fact was not the point; what matters is that the *Québecois* of the day thought this way.

The war did nothing to ameliorate the situation. Sam Hughes was a Minister of Militia of wondrous energy and drive, but he was not the man best calculated to win the hearts of *la belle province*. Hughes was an Orangeman, and as such he was viewed as a rabid Protestant by Roman Catholic French Canadians. He made the mistake of appointing a Protestant clergyman to supervise recruiting in Quebec, and he was continually exhorting French Canadians to fight for France, as if France was to French Canada as England was to English Canada.

Equally important, Hughes did nothing to assuage the martial pride of the province. Only one French-Canadian regiment was sent overseas to fight at the front—the 22nd, the famous Van-Doos—and few senior officers who were French-speaking received important posts. It seemed to hypersensitive Quebec as if the province was once again being cheated.

To be sure, there were many in the province who did not care if the French Canadian received anything from the war. The less they had to do with the whole business, the better. These *nationalistes* were led by Henri Bourassa, the brilliant editor of the Montreal newspaper, *Le Devoir*, and one of the great orators of Canadian history. Bourassa was a French Canadian, but he was more; he was a Canadian. He believed that Canada should be independent from Britain, freed from the apron strings of Mother England. Canada, he said, had gone to war not for reasons of her own, but simply and only because Britain was at war. This was colonialism of the most abject kind as far as Bourassa was concerned.

Moderate French-Canadian opinion was best represented by Sir Wilfrid Laurier, the leader of the Liberal party. Prime Minister from 1896 to 1911, Laurier was a beloved figure to millions of Canadians. He was a politician and a partisan politician, but he seemed at the same time to be a gentleman, a man of honour, and the personification of the best hopes for Canada. As one of his biographers, Joseph Schull, has called him, he was "The First Canadian."[3]

But Laurier had been defeated in 1911 by the Conservatives under Sir Robert Borden. Borden was a Nova Scotian, a man with enormous patience and perseverance but no brilliance. He had taken office on the strength of the backlash against Laurier's proposed reciprocity agreement with the United States; the agreement, Tories charged, would lead inevitably to the annexation of Canada by her neighbour to the south. In Quebec, Laurier had been hurt severely by the nationalists who claimed that he had sold out to the English-speaking Canadians. Obviously, Laurier as a French Canadian was considered by the English as a man who had no ties to Britain and who would not hesitate to sell out Canada to the Americans; to French Canadians, he was seen as a man who had made too many compromises with the majority race and who was, as a result, in the pocket of the English. The position of a French-Canadian prime minister was difficult indeed.

But now the problem was Borden's. The Quebec nationalists had joined with the Conservatives to defeat Laurier, and Borden had the task of keeping them in harness with his English-speaking supporters. This task became more difficult as the Great

War dragged on and on and as the casualties mounted ever higher.

The root of the problem was that the French Canadians simply were not enlisting. In his New Year's Day Message of 1916, Borden had promised that Canada would enlist an army of 500,000 men. This was a very large force for a country of only 8 million inhabitants, and the total could not be reached if the 2.5 million French Canadians did not contribute their "share" of men for the bloodbath in Flanders. But there were few signs that the French Canadians were going to start volunteering in any large numbers.

To Quebec the real war in 1915 and 1916 was the war in Ontario, and the casualties were the French-Canadian children who were threatened with the loss of their language. This, and not the battle fronts of Europe, was the focus of Quebec eyes. The English of Ontario, charged the French-language press, were the Prussians of Canada. Not a man for Europe until the war in Ontario was won!

The battle of the Ontario schools question was fought in the House of Commons at Ottawa and in Borden's cabinet. But the problem was one for the Province of Ontario, not for the federal parliament, and there was little that could be done even had Borden wanted to act. Certainly the Ontario government was adamant in its refusal to alter its education regulations, correctly claiming that the voters of the province would eject from office any government that catered to the French. The tragedy was that the breach between the two Canadian races was widening at a time when the demands of the war should have been bringing them closer.

By 1916, French-English relations were at their lowest point since the hanging of Riel in 1885. The French Canadians were assailed in Ontario and the west as a cowardly race who would not fight. Racial and religious slurs were hurled at the Province of Quebec, and even moderate English-Canadian opinion was reaching the boiling point. Demands were beginning to be heard for a system that would equalize sacrifice at the war fronts —conscription. If the French would not volunteer, then they should be made to fight.

CONSCRIPTION BECOMES POLICY

Borden did not believe in conscription. He could see that the political difficulties involved would probably outweigh the extra men raised. And he was fully aware that French-Canadian opinion of all political hues was vehemently opposed to anything that smacked of compulsion. No, conscription was not the answer.

But the question of getting enough men for the army was still there. The simple fact of the matter is that the Great War was badly run in Canada—and almost everywhere. No one knew how many men were available and physically fit for overseas service. No one knew how many farmers had to be kept on the land in order to produce food necessary for home consumption and to supply the Allied nations. No one knew how many industrial workers were required to produce the enormous quantities of ammunition, armaments, and equipment needed by the armies overseas. Without this information, how could the war be properly run? Clearly, it could not.

The result was a national registration conducted in late 1916 and early 1917. Citizens were asked to fill in a form listing their various skills and talents, and briefly indicating their physical condition. But the return of the forms was purely voluntary; as a result, only incomplete information was obtained. With the techniques of 1916-17, too, it took months of work to tabulate the information received, and when this task was completed conscription for overseas service had already been introduced.

Borden gave notice of his intention to introduce conscription legislation in May, 1917, a few days after his return from the United Kingdom. Why had he changed his mind? There were several reasons. The war was going badly for the Allies, and it was not beyond the realm of possibility that the Germans could win. Men were needed in ever increasing numbers by the armies, for casualties were huge in number in the trench-war conditions in France. Most important, from Borden's point of view, was the fact that volunteers were not coming forward in sufficient numbers to permit the Canadian troops at the front to be reinforced up to fighting strength.

These were the military reasons behind Borden's switch, but there were also several political reasons. The Americans had at last entered the war in April, 1917, and there was a clear calculation on the part of certain Empire statesmen that the "Yanks" should not be permitted to feel that they had saved the Allies. The Empire troops had to be maintained at strength so that the Empire bargaining position at the peace conference would be preserved. Borden had also been working to increase the independence of Canada within the Empire, and he realized that the dominion's war effort was the best guarantee that he would see his case conceded. And finally, an election in Canada was a near-certainty for 1917. Although he was aware of the difficulties involved in conscription, Borden might well have realized that it would be better for him to appear before the electors as the advocate of a greater war effort—as the advocate of conscription —than for him to stand for re-election only on his government's record.

These reasons sound terribly cynical, but they were not. Politicians have to be in office to achieve their ends, and to stay in office they must win elections. But the best proof of Borden's sincerity is that he approached Laurier at the end of May, 1917 and asked him to join in a coalition government, offering the Liberal chief half the portfolios in the cabinet for his party and the premiership for himself if he so desired. The only catch was that the coalition would be formed to introduce conscription.

The choice was agonizing for Laurier. He was being offered more than a fair share of power if he would help to implement conscription. But Laurier knew that his own people were dead-set against compulsion, and the old leader could see his hold over the Province of Quebec destroyed and power passing to the nationalists if he agreed. This was something he was not prepared to accept, and Laurier turned down Borden's offer.

For Borden, this was a setback, but he proceeded with his conscription bill in parliament. Sentiment in English Canada was very strongly in favour of this legislation, and soon Borden could see cracks in the Liberal ranks as English-speaking Grits began to grow restive in the face of Laurier's resistance to conscription. When Borden introduced two further bills, one providing for the taking of the soldiers' vote overseas and the other for the disfranchisement of aliens and the enfranchisement of soldiers' relatives, the cracks in Liberalism turned into gaping chasms. The aliens' bill took away the vote of a segment of the population that had been Liberal in overwhelming numbers. It gave the vote to wives, mothers and daughters of soldiers, women who could be expected to support any government that promised to do things for their loved ones in Flanders. The vote was being gerrymandered so that the government could not lose.

The English-speaking Liberals in parliament could see the writing on the wall, and with few exceptions they deserted Laurier. By October, Borden had his Union Government, including key provincial Liberals from Ontario and the west, and representatives from the federal party. Laurier was left with a handful of English Liberals and his massed Quebec supporters. The split along racial lines that had been feared for so long had finally occurred. English Canada and French Canada were lined up on solidly opposed positions.

The general election of December, 1917 confirmed the break in relations. The Union Government pulled out all the stops to defeat the Laurier Liberals. "Who would the Kaiser vote for?," the electorate was asked. The Liberals, the charges went, would let down the boys at the front. To ensure the victory, the government offered exemptions from conscription to farmers, many of whom had previously been prepared to oppose the Union Government. In Quebec, Laurier was supported by the *nationalistes* who had opposed him six years earlier; but this too added fuel to the Union Government campaign in English Canada. Bourassa, who was regarded there as something close to the Anti-Christ, was little help to Laurier outside Quebec. The results of the voting saw the Borden government returned with an overwhelming majority from English Canada—and with scarcely a seat in Quebec.

THE AFTERMATH OF CONSCRIPTION

The voters had confirmed their acceptance of conscription. But despite the very real need for men that had impelled Borden to ask for this legislation in May, 1917, the call-up of conscripts did not begin until the New Year, and only some 45,000 draftees reached the battlefields. National disunity was a high price to pay for 45,000 men.

And there was disunity. There were riots in Quebec City and Montreal against the conscription act. The farmers of English Canada and Quebec marched on Ottawa in May, 1918 after the pledged exemptions for farmers' sons were cancelled. Aliens resented bitterly that their votes had been taken away. It was an unhappy nation that saw the war of exhaustion in Europe come to an end in November, 1918.

More than 60,000 Canadians did not return from the battlefields of Europe. The sacrifice of the best men of their generation on the altar of European diplomacy is something from which Canada has not yet recovered. There was scarcely a home in the land that was not affected in some way by the war. Because of this deep hurt, the pain and racial bitterness of the war years lingered on into the peace.

The selection of new leaders by the Liberals and Conservatives did nothing to bind up the wounds. The Conservative-Unionist party selected Arthur Meighen as Sir Robert Borden's successor. Meighen had drafted the Military Service Act, the conscription legislation of 1917, and he had led the fight in the House of Commons that had rammed the bill through over the opposition of the Liberals. Meighen was a brilliant orator, an intellect of the first order, but no politician. Once his mind was made up on an issue, nothing would or could shake his convictions. His policy had been reached after careful reasoning; it had to be right. This had been the rationale for his support of conscription in 1917, but with this on his own record how could he hope to win support in Quebec?

The Liberals' choice to succeed Laurier was a man of different stamp, William Lyon Mackenzie King. King was a pudgy little man, dumpy in appearance. He was cautious and careful, intelligent and very, very, shrewd. One of the few English-speaking Liberals of stature who had stayed loyal to Laurier, King could count on the support of Quebec. And he got it time after time. But more important, King set out deliberately with the intention of bringing back into the party those men who had felt compelled to support conscription. King was trying to bind up the wounds of the Liberal party.

Mackenzie King would soon have his chance to begin to bind up the wounds of the nation. The Union Government staggered into the 1920's in deep disarray. Meighen was not a Prime Minister who could keep his mixed bag of Liberals and Conservatives together without an emotional issue such as conscription as cement. The election of 1921 saw Meighen driven from office and the Liberals re-installed in power after ten years in the wilderness.

The election had been a bitter one. In Quebec, the Liberals attacked Meighen viciously as the architect of conscription, portraying him with bloody hands from the carnage of Flanders. The French-language press was particularly virulent in its attacks, flogging what the Governor General, Lord Byng of Vimy, privately called "an extremely dead horse. . . . Conscription."[4] The election, one of Meighen's correspondents said, "was principally run on Laurier's grave. . . ."[5] But there was another side to this disagreeable tale. The Conservatives in English Canada portrayed the Liberals as the party of Quebec, raising the claim that if King was returned Quebec would dominate. Even charges that Mackenzie King was a slacker because he had not enlisted during the war were widespread throughout the country. What kind of a soldier King would have made—he was forty years old in 1914—was left unclear. The Liberals, to their credit, did not raise the fact that Meighen too had not enlisted.

Again in the federal elections of 1925 and 1926 the "conscription bogey" was raised. And both times Meighen suffered outrageous attacks in Quebec. To the French Canadians Meighen was the embodiment of the worst characteristics of English Canada: imperialistic, narrow minded, rigid, cold. Not until the Conservatives had a new leader in the person of R. B. Bennett did Quebec start to forgive and forget. In the election of 1930, the Conservatives won twenty-four seats in Quebec and a national majority.

*   *   *

By 1935, the situation in Europe was such that war was once more a possibility. Hitler was in power in Germany and his nation was rearming at a furious rate. Fascist Italy had just overrun Ethiopia. Japan was ravaging China. Perhaps conscription could have become an issue in the general election of 1935. The signs were all there. But with the Great Depression still holding Canada in its grasp, all other issues paled into insignificance. King was re-elected with an enormous mandate after a campaign run without a platform. He had not needed one.

But the memory of conscription still existed. In the mind of Quebec it was a real subject still, the time when the naked power of the majority had been brutally employed. For English Canadians, conscription was something about which many felt embarrassed. The rigging of the vote and the violation of the compact of 1867 were not acts about which one could be proud. But, thought many English-speaking people, conscription had been necessary. And if the circumstances should ever rise again. . . .

Chapter II

To War Again

Mackenzie King was a most complex man. In 1939 he had been leader of the Liberal Party for twenty years and Prime Minister for more than twelve. Nevertheless, he remained virtually unknown to his people, to his colleagues, and to his opponents. Unknown, yes; admired in some respects, yes; liked, perhaps; but loved, never.

PERSONALITIES, PARTIES AND POLICIES

King had no ability to arouse in his supporters a love and loyalty such as Laurier could. One press reporter wrote to a friend in 1923, just two years after King had first become Prime Minister:

> One can never tell what King will do. He is such a pompous ass that an orangoutang that would flatter him could choose its own reward.[1]

In 1941, one of King's closer colleagues was reported to be equally critical of his leader:

> . . . he simply can't stand the worm at close quarters—bad breath, a fetid, unhealthy, sinister atmosphere, like living close to some filthy object.

However, this observer was fair enough to add, "get off a piece and he looks better and better. . . ."[2]

This is the key to understanding Mackenzie King and the way he ran the war effort from 1939 to 1945. Examined in isolation, his acts do not always seem entirely honourable. Studied without reference to the broader context, his treatment of individuals was sometimes shockingly callous and even brutal. But stand off a piece, and he looks better and better. Mackenzie King was a lonely man, virtually friendless except for his pet dog and one or two people with whom he corresponded freely. His personality almost certainly cannot be understood by anyone without training in psychology. He was no crackpot, however, and the Prime Minister knew very well where he was headed at all times.

Where was he headed? What was his goal? There can be no doubt about this. To King, the great need in Canada was for unity, for harmony between the English-and French-speaking Canadian. To this he dedicated himself. The American Minister in Ottawa in 1940, J. Pierrepont Moffat, commented on this aspect of Mackenzie King's career in a long despatch to the State Department in December, 1940:

> Alone among the outstanding British Canadian leaders today, Mr. Mackenzie King trusts, and consequently is trusted by, the French Canadian. He views national unity, not as a means but as an end. He will delay, he will compromise, he will travel only part of the road he would follow if he can travel with French and British Canadians pulling in double harness. For this he is often bitterly blamed by the Imperialists in Canada, but their criticism does not deflect him. He has seen the mistakes of the past, and what is rare, he has learned from them. . . .
> In this I acquit Mr. King of any self-interest or political opportunism. His vision of a united Canada is a very genuine one, with almost a mystic tinge. It is one of the many things he *feels*, where his power of expression is less vivid than the feeling itself.[3]

Without national unity, there was no hope for Canada. Nothing, Mackenzie King believed, could be allowed to destroy this.

Behind him, Mackenzie King mustered a huge majority in the House of Commons and a vigorous, well-financed, Liberal party machine. The party was in control of the provincial legislatures in seven of the nine provinces, Alberta and Quebec being the exceptions. Most important, perhaps, the Liberals were the only truly national party on the federal level, with strong representation in every region of the country.

In French Canada, the party held a stranglehold, its members occupying sixty of the province's sixty-five seats at Ottawa. The key men there for the Liberals were P. J. A. Cardin, the Minister of Public Works, C. G. (Chubby) Power, the Minister of Pensions and National Health and a key party organizer, and Ernest Lapointe, the Minister of Justice. Lapointe was King's right-hand man, shrewd, calculating, and a tower of integrity. For all practical purposes he ran the Liberal party in French Canada, and on issues involving relations between French and English Canadians his word carried great weight with the Prime Minister.

Against the towering strength of the Liberals, the Conservative party could rally only a corporal's guard. The party had

The Right Honourable Ernest Lapointe, Ottawa, 1941.

"He was gigantic of figure. . . . His mind matched his body in magnitude. He had come to Parliament early in the century without a word of English, had painfully taught it to himself, and now, with a fascinating inflection and a quaint misuse of words, was almost as good an orator in English as Meighen, almost Laurier's equal in French. As a human being he was several sizes larger than King."

Bruce Hutchison, *The Incredible Canadian* (Toronto: Longmans, Green, 1952), p. 63.

elected only forty Members of Parliament in 1935, twenty-five from Ontario, and five from Quebec, all English-speaking. In addition, the party was desperately short of money—as late as 1939 there was a large debt outstanding from the 1935 election —and without funds almost no organizational work could be undertaken.

But there were signs of change. In the summer of 1938, the party had selected a new leader to replace Richard B. Bennett, and they looked to him to rejuvenate the party throughout the country and especially in Quebec. The new Tory chief was Dr. Robert J. Manion, an amiable physician from Fort William, Ontario. Manion was a good man, honest, friendly, loyal, but he had made many enemies in his political career. Unfortunately for him a large number of these enemies were too powerfully entrenched in the Conservative party to be easily dislodged.

The major issue for the Conservatives was how Canada should react if there were to be another war in Europe and Britain became involved. Indeed this was a major issue throughout the country from 1938 on. Some, a small but relatively influential group of academics and some politicians, believed that Canada should stay neutral. Why, they asked, should the new world be required to go forth once a generation to rescue Europe from its follies? Very few Conservatives held views like this. Most stated simply that when Britain was at war, Canada was at war. In the middle was Bob Manion who was desperately trying to win a foothold in Quebec for his party.

Quebec Conservatives and most French-speaking Canadians whatever their party would generally have preferred to see Canada stay out of European wars. They were realistic enough to realize, however, that this was highly unlikely, if only because English-speaking Canadians formed the majority of the population. In the light of this cold fact, the Canadien agreed reluctantly that Canada could participate but only in a limited way. Canada could send economic aid and volunteers, he said, but there could be no conscription for overseas service under any circumstances. Never again would there be a 1917 situation.

Manion was prepared to accept this approach, although there were many Conservatives who disagreed with him. These men included Arthur Meighen, the architect of the conscription bill of 1917 and two-time prime minister during the 1920's, and a host of lesser lights. The only way to fight a war, these men believed, was with conscription. Any other method was unfair, unjust, and bore too heavily on the classes who could least be spared. In addition, to deny the necessity for conscription was to say that 1917 had been a mistake, to admit that Borden and Meighen were wrong. This was something they could never do.

Nonetheless, Manion determined to act, and on March 27, 1939 he announced against conscription. He told the press in Ottawa:

> I do not believe that Canadian youth should be conscripted to fight outside the borders of Canada. Canada can play her full part in the Empire and in support of our democratic institutions by full co-operation with Great Britain through volunteer units, through supplying munitions, foods and other necessities to our allies, and by fully protecting Canada's own territory.[4]

Three days later, Mackenzie King, too, came down flatly against overseas conscription:

> Let me say that so long as this government may be in power, no such measure will be enacted.[5]

Both great parties were now on record against conscription and in favour of voluntary participation, the policy that Canada in fact was to follow for the first five years of the Second World War.

Historically more aware of the need to maintain harmonious relations between the Canadian language groups, the Liberal party developed few apparent strains over this no-conscription policy. The Conservatives, however, began to be torn apart on the question. One Toronto Tory said:

> I am very disappointed in Manion's leadership, because he will not take a stand without first considering what the attitude of Quebec will be, so that in essence he allows

Quebec to determine his policy and in that respect is following the lead of King. . . .[6]

This was an attitude widely shared among English-Canadian Conservatives. Unfortunately for Manion, his Quebec followers were also dissatisfied. Their position was understandable. Trying to crack the Liberal stronghold, they had to be able to offer more than their opponents. What they wanted was that Manion should declare against any automatic commitment by Canada to Britain in the event of war.

This attitude puzzled the harassed Conservative leader. He wrote to one French Canadian:

> I do not see any reason why I must, every time I open my mouth, talk of this damned issue . . . and quite frankly, I don't see why so many of you chaps down there find it necessary to talk all the time on questions of this kind.[7]

It seems clear that neither Manion nor his Quebec supporters really understood the position of the other. Manion had already gone further than prudence should have dictated, so far in fact that he was threatened with the loss of some of his supporters in Ontario and British Columbia. But the Quebec *bleus*, too, were in a difficult position, subject to attack from every platform with the Conservative record from the Great War. The party's dilemma was probably insoluble.

The entire discussion about the issue of war participation and conscription, of course, had taken place in peacetime conditions. That war was coming, however, few could doubt. The Munich agreement in the fall of 1938 had bought time, but Nazi Germany continued its pressure upon Czechoslovakia and Poland. The Czechs were swallowed up in March, 1939, and Poland was next. The German tanks crossed the frontier on September 1. A British and French ultimatum remained unanswered, and on September 3, 1939, Britain declared war on Germany. The polite sparring in Canada had come to an end. Now the emotional issues of participation and conscription would have to be fought out in the midst of a war.

To War Again ❖ 17

WAR DECLARED

Mackenzie King's understanding of the Canadian mentality was never better demonstrated than in the first days of September, 1939. For all practical purposes, the Canadian rearmament program of the late 1930's had been undertaken on the assumption that Canada would participate alongside Britain in any new war, and after the fall of 1938, the Prime Minister had been certain that Canada would soon have to do so. But he had promised on innumerable occasions that parliament would decide the nation's course on peace or war. How could he keep his promise without alienating die-hard imperialists, neutralists, and French-Canadian nationalists?

His solution was masterful. As early as August 25, the Prime Minister announced that "precautionary measures" would be taken, and the militia was called out to guard strategic points. On September 1, a Canadian Active Service Force was mobilized, and after Britain declared war "all necessary measures which would be required in a state of war" were taken.[8] Officially, however, Canada was not yet in a state of war. On September 7, a special session of parliament assembled to hear the Governor General declare that it had been summoned "in order that the government may seek authority for the measures necessary for the defence of Canada, and for cooperation in the determined effort . . . to resist further aggression. . . ."[9] The following day King repeated his promises against conscription, but not until September 9 did he make it clear that, if the House was willing, the government would take immediate steps for the issue of a declaration of war against Germany.

This calculated policy of indecision seemed to disarm critics of government policy. An attempt by Liguori Lacombe, an isolationist Liberal M.P. from Quebec, to have the House of Commons declare that "Canada should refrain from participating in war outside Canada"[10] was rejected without a vote, and the government was given a free hand. A formal submission was despatched to King George VI in London on September 9, and the next day Canada was at war with Nazi Germany. Some imperialist Members of Parliament claimed that this whole procedure was unnecessary, stating as did Tommy Church, a true blue Tory from Toronto, that "it is well known that when Britain is at war Canada is at war."[11] One or two Quebec newspapers took the opposite tack, demanding neutrality on the grounds that it was not Canada's fight. But the opposition was minor, and the Governor General, Lord Tweedsmuir, noted that, "My Prime Minister has succeeded very skillfully, in aligning Canada alongside Britain with a minimum of disturbance.[12] King's policy of insisting that parliament would decide had brought a virtually unanimous country into the war.

A unanimous country, yes, but not a happy country. There were no fiery speeches, no bands, no pretty girls throwing flowers before the troops. No one said that the Allies would be in Berlin in a week, and very few expected anything but a long dirty war. Canada had entered the Second World War fully aware of the sacrifices that would be necessary. And it should be stressed that Canada had also entered the war on several clear understandings. First and foremost, there would be no conscription for overseas service. This was a pledge that had been made by both Liberals and Conservatives, and it was this pledge that brought Quebec into the war, albeit reluctantly. Secondly, there was an unspoken agreement that the war effort would be a limited one, that Canada would not pour out her blood and treasure as she had from 1914 to 1918.

Could any country fight a limited war? This was a difficult question. In September, 1939, however, it seemed fully possible for Canada to do so. The British were not interested in large numbers of troops, and there was no expectation that Canada could provide them. Even R. B. Bennett, the former Prime Minister and a keen imperialist, was aware of this, as he indicated in a letter to his brother-in-law:

> No one knows better than you that Canada cannot send across any such numbers as were sent during the last war, and in any event she should not do so. . . . What England wants is a place to train men, and plants to manufacture machines which are capable of being flown across the Atlantic Ocean.[13]

Certainly this was the government's understanding, too. Canada's major contribution was to be economic. Next in importance would be the British Commonwealth Air Training Plan, under the terms of which Canada would make available her vast spaces so that airmen could be trained in the skills of war. Third, and much the least in importance, would be the contribution of ground troops to the Allied armies. In discussions with Major-General A. G. L. McNaughton, the officer selected for the command of the First Canadian Division, the Minister of National Defence, Norman Rogers, made it very clear that financial and other reasons would limit the scope of the Canadian contribution.[14] Nonetheless, the division was prepared with speed, and on December 10 the first convoys left for Great Britain.

Had the war in Europe not developed into a "phoney war," there might have been sharp demands for a greater contribution made on the King government. But after Poland was crushed, the Germans went into winter quarters, and the Allied armies faced the Nazis over the Maginot Line. Few skirmishes of any significance were reported, and casualties were light. The troops sang ditties about hanging out their washing on the Siegfried Line, the German defence network, but the generals stayed silent in the rear area dugouts. The most serious challenges to Canadian arms in these first months of war came from Quebec and Ontario.

POLITICS IN THE PROVINCES

The Premier of Quebec when the war began was Maurice Duplessis, the leader of the Union Nationale party. His party had originally been formed by a coalition of reform groups, but after Duplessis had led them to power in 1936 the reform elements had been driven from the government. The Duplessis regime had soon become obsessed with preserving its autonomy from Ottawa and interested chiefly in selling its resources to English-Canadian and American corporations. With his seventy-five members in the ninety-man legislature, Duplessis seemed safe. But the war seemed to provide *Le Chef* with an opportunity to renew his mandate and strike yet another blow for Quebec autonomy.

Duplessis' plan was to fight his provincial election against the Mackenzie King government, attacking the Prime Minister for using the war as an excuse to destroy the autonomy of the provinces. Duplessis' manifesto claimed:

> Using the pretext of a war declared by the federal government, the campaign of assimilation and centralization that had been evident for several years increased in an intolerable fashion. . . . [The Union Nationale] would work unceasingly and work always on projects of construction and reconstruction, but never on projects of destruction.[15]

The gauntlet had been hurled in Ottawa's face. If its authority and if its war effort were to be maintained, the King government could not afford to ignore the challenge.

Mackenzie King and the French-speaking, federal cabinet members from Quebec were hesitant at first about tussling with the Union Nationale on ground of the latter's own choosing. In these circumstances, it was "Chubby" Power, the tough little Irishman from Quebec City, who swung the decisive weight. Power later wrote:

> I argued that there was nothing for us to do but to accept the challenge, and openly and boldly take part in the election. Within a very short time I came to the further conclusion that our hands would be immensely strengthened if, in addition to a declaration of participation in the provincial election, we stated that the challenge was such that unless the province rejected Duplessis, and by this means gave its approval of our action in support of Canada's war effort, we would be obliged to resign our portfolios and retire to the status of private members.[16]

In other words, either Quebec tossed out Duplessis or the Quebec members of the federal cabinet would resign and leave the province to the mercy of the English-Canadian conscriptionists.

This was a daring gamble. But once committed to the fight the Liberals went all-out to beat Duplessis. Money was poured into the province from all across the country; the federal party openly took over and ran the provincial campaign; and explicit, absolute, unambiguous pledges of opposition to conscription

Camillien Houde (left) and Maurice Duplessis. Houde, at one time leader of the Quebec Conservative party, was mayor of Montreal from 1928 to 1954 except for brief intervals. Between 1940 and 1944 he was interned for open defiance of the 1940 National Registration Act. (See page 29.)

"Houde . . . born of poor parents in the city of Montreal, was a product of his rough, tough early environment. He looked like what he pretended to be, a man of the people. . . . He was extremely clever, with great oratorical powers, forceful and even violent in his discourses."

". . . Duplessis, having found himself in considerable difficulty, in part because of his own recklessness in administration and his arrogant and sometimes abusive attitude towards the financial interests, was endeavouring to cover the deficiencies of his administration by deliberately diverting the public interest from provincial matters to those concerning the Canadian nation as a whole. He saw in the declaration of war by the Canadian government an opportunity to take what might be called an electoral gamble. . . ."

Norman Ward (ed.), *A Party Politician: The Memoirs of Chubby Power* (Toronto: Macmillan, 1966), pp. 323, 346.

were made by Power, Ernest Lapointe, P. J. A. Cardin and Adélard Godbout, the leader of the Quebec Liberal party. Godbout, for example, stated the issue flatly in a radio address:

> I undertake on my honour, weighing each of my words, to quit my party and to fight it if a single French Canadian from now to the end of hostilities in Europe is mobilized against his will under a Liberal government or under a provisional government in which members of the Rt. Hon. Mr. King's cabinet participate.[17]

Godbout would live to regret those words, but in October, 1939 they had a striking effect.

The result of the election on October 25 was a dramatic turnover of seats from the Union Nationale to the Liberals. Godbout's party won 53 percent of the popular vote and sixty-nine seats. Duplessis was crushed, and Ottawa had won. English-speaking Canadians too readily assumed that the victory meant Quebec was solidly in favour of the war, that the nation was united. This was perhaps one lesson from the Quebec election. But the important lesson went largely unremarked: Quebec had decided that it could best protect itself from conscription by having a strong group of cabinet ministers in Ottawa. Duplessis could do nothing to prevent conscription, the *Québecois* had decided, but Lapointe, Cardin and Power could.

The respite from political strife after Duplessis' defeat was brief, lasting just over two months. Then it was Ontario's turn to disrupt affairs and upset political applecarts. The issue as it turned out was almost the direct opposite of that raised by Duplessis. Instead of doing too much, Ontario leaders charged that Mackenzie King was doing too little. Ottawa was fighting a slacker's war.

Mitchell Hepburn, the Ontario Premier, had been feuding with Mackenzie King for years. Shrewd, tough, bouncy, Hepburn had single-handedly put the Liberals into power in Ontario in 1934. Talking reform and pledging to clean up the waste of years of Tory governments, he swept into office on the strength of a dynamic campaign and his own personal magnetism. But once in power, his career had followed a similiar path to that of Maurice Duplessis. Reform was soon forgotten, and the new broom that should have swept clean was put away; the *status quo* remained undisturbed. Soon King and Hepburn were fighting each other with as much vigour as either had ever shown in taking on the Tories. By 1938, all but formal relations between the two Liberals had virtually ceased.

When "Mitch" Hepburn rose in the Ontario legislature in January, 1940, his attacks on the King government were not entirely unexpected. What the Premier had never done before, however, was to move an actual motion of censure against Ottawa. This was news. The King administration, Hepburn charged, was guilty of slipshod measures and a lack of energy in the prosecution of the war. Privately, Hepburn was also writing of his disgust at finding soldiers "without uniforms, proper underwear and shoes" in a Toronto camp.[18] The Hepburn motion was blasted through the legislature with a vote of forty-four to ten, as the opposition Conservatives, led by George Drew who was if anything a more vehement critic of the government than Hepburn, joined in. Only ten Ontario Liberals were courageous enough to resist their Premier and support their national party leader.

THE ELECTION OF 1940

The Hepburn-Drew resolution gave Mackenzie King an opportunity that he had been looking for. Now he could avoid holding a session of parliament, a session that was sure to be a difficult one because an election was known to be coming in 1940. Unfortunately, King had promised Manion that he would have a session of parliament before dissolution, but the extraordinary Ontario resolution justified abandoning this pledge—or so King believed. King believed that his government was "in a very strong position from one end of the country to the other. That Hepburn's action is on all fours with Duplessis'. That he has been living in an atmosphere of groups around him in Toronto; is filled with his own prejudice and hate. . . ." And King added with a shrewd awareness:

> . . . the greatest relief of all is the probability of having the election over before the worst of the fighting begins in Europe. I have dreaded having to choose the moment for

Ontario's Liberal Premier, Mitchell Hepburn (right), and the
Conservative Leader of the Opposition, George Drew.

". . . the informal alliance between Hepburn and Drew was
strengthened after Drew became leader of the Ontario
Conservatives. As Drew wrote to Manion in the summer of
1939, the resulting situation was unique in Canadian political
history. He would attack Hepburn if it served the interests
of the national party, Drew said, but he believed there was
much to gain by letting the Ontario Premier devote his
energies to attacking Mackenzie King."

J. L. Granatstein, *The Politics of Survival: The Conservative
Party of Canada, 1939-45* (Toronto: University of Toronto
Press, 1967), p. 38.

the campaign and specially to choose it at a time when
human lives are being slaughtered by hundreds of thousands, if not by millions.[19]

King's bombshell was revealed on January 25, 1940, the day
that parliament met for the 1940 session. The announcement
that the government had decided on an "immediate appeal

to the country" left the opposition stunned. Mackenzie King placed the blame squarely on the heads of Mitchell Hepburn and George Drew and watched his opponents squirm uncomfortably. The Conservatives were desperately short of money, and their attempts at reorganization, while under way, still needed several months to come to fruition. The Co-operative Commonwealth Federation was still only a tiny group of socialists, and their support was badly split on the question of just how Canada should aid the Allies. Mackenzie King clearly had stolen a march on his opponents.

To recover their lost ground, the Conservatives needed an issue, and they thought they had found it when Dr. Manion announced that he favoured a "truly national government in the sense that the very best brains obtainable among our people are drafted to serve in the Cabinet." If elected, the Conservative leader promised, "I shall form such a government."[20] Superficially, the idea of a national government was very appealing. What could be more logical than to submerge party differences and fight the war under the leadership of men whose only aim was victory? What could be more sensible than to open the highest posts in the land to men of ability from businesses and universities, men who would not normally go into politics?

On the other hand, there were severe drawbacks in selling a national government to the people. French Canadians hearing the phrase thought instinctively of Union Government, and to Canadiens this was synonymous with conscription. This was a bad start in itself, but when Quebeckers saw that it was the Conservative party which called for national government, their darkest suspicions were confirmed. Manion's call for national government, they believed, was a Tory plot to secure conscription by the back door. Manion and Meighen, they must have believed, were much the same.

Curiously, perhaps, French Canadians were not alone in associating the Conservatives and their national government plank with conscription. The simple fact is that almost no one in Canada favoured compulsory service in the winter of 1940. Before every meeting, Manion later recalled, "the first demand by our candidates was that I make it very clear I was opposed to conscription for overseas service."[21] But the strain of 1917 was too dark to wash away with repeated pledges. There can be no doubt that the most effective weapon against the Conservative party in the 1940 election was the belief that it was too imperialistic, too aggressive, too likely to press for conscription. Too many Canadians apparently remembered the casualties, the suffering, the internal strife of the Great War.

The Liberals benefited from this trend. It seemed that few Canadians could envisage Mackenzie King as the great war leader, mobilizing men and machines. And it seemed that the colourless King was precisely what the country wanted in 1940. He was safe, he was slow, he was cautious. Above all, Canadians were afraid of another racial split on the lines of 1917, and who was the man best qualified to prevent this? Who had devoted his life to national unity? Who indeed, if not Mackenzie King? All these themes were summed up in a Liberal advertisement in the *Halifax Chronicle* on March 25, 1940:

> Canada Needs King
> A United Canada Will Spur Britain on to Victory
> A Liberal Vote is a Win the War Vote

Mackenzie King, the advertisement concluded, is "Experienced, Dependable, Resolute, Energetic, Patriotic and above all Efficient."

The result of the election on March 26, 1940 was a landslide of unprecedented proportions for the Liberals. Only forty Conservatives were elected as against 184 Liberals, the largest majority to that time. The CCF returned eight members and the New Democracy, a group of Social Crediters from Alberta, ten. Mackenzie King had his mandate. The war was his to run.

The first casualty of the 1940 election was Robert Manion, the Conservative leader. Everyone liked Bob Manion, but he had not produced the goods. It made no difference that the party had wanted national government as an issue. It made no difference that Manion had been beaten by the master strategist in Canadian political history. He had to go. To many Conservatives of an imperialist hue, it was a good thing that he should be replaced. Manion was soft on Quebec, and he was against conscription. In wartime—and notwithstanding the results of the election—these were disqualifications. Manion was succeeded by Richard Hanson, a Fredericton lawyer and a former minister in the cabinet of R. B. Bennett. Hanson was stolid, dull, heavy, but he was a political realist. He would have to lead the Conservatives through the new situation that was sprung on the world after May 10, 1940.

The "phoney war" was over. In a series of lightning assaults, the Nazi legions crashed their way through Holland and Belgium, outflanking the French defences. The Allied armies were sent reeling back, and it took a miracle of no mean proportions to save the British Expeditionary Force at Dunkirk. In little more than a month the world situation was transformed. France was occupied by the Germans, and Britain was virtually alone against the *Wehrmacht*. From being a minor character in a cast of thousands, Canada suddenly was flung onto stage centre. Almost overnight Canada had become Britain's ranking ally.

*   *   *

The terrifying events of May and June burst on a shocked public in Canada. Almost immediately there were demands that Mackenzie King should step down and make way for a war leader, for a Canadian Churchill. One Conservative Member of Parliament told the House of Commons:

> The greatest contribution you can make towards winning the war, Mr. Prime Minister, is for you to hand in your resignation.[22]

There was no chance that King would do this, but there was no doubt that extraordinary actions would have to be taken.

King's response was to pass the National Resources Mobilization Act (NRMA). This act was an extraordinarily broad piece of legislation, authorizing "special emergency powers to permit the mobilization of all the effective resources of the nation, both human and material, for the purpose of the defence and security of Canada."[23] The idea, in part at least, had been suggested by Conservative leader Hanson in a private meeting with King. But Hanson had also wanted conscription for overseas service, something that King refused to give. The Prime Minister, however, did agree to the conscription of young men for service in Canada, and this was the primary result of NRMA. The first step on the long road to full conscription had been taken.

Chapter III

The First Conscription Crisis: 1942

The national reaction to the introduction of conscription for Canadian service was surprisingly placid. There were only a few cries from English Canadians for total conscription, and the response from Quebec was moderate. Ernest Lapointe had agreed to the NRMA willingly—the defence of Canada was as much a subject of concern to French Canadians as to anyone —and even the extremists were quiet. Camilien Houde, the Mayor of Montreal, stirred up a bit of a fuss by urging his compatriots to refuse to comply with the government's National Registration of August, 1940, but he was soon interned for the duration. Even locking up Houde roused few protests—although civil libertarians should have been concerned—and the reaction of the French-language press was that Houde had received what he deserved.

By October the first conscripts in the twenty-one to twenty-four year age groups had been called up for service. The initial period of service was only for thirty days, barely enough to teach even the fundamentals of soldiering. The reasons for the short training period were clear: there were no modern weapons available. The fall of France had left Britain denuded in the face of the enemy and every serviceable weapon had been rushed overseas. In addition, no one had contemplated that the raising of large numbers of men for home defence in Canada would be necessary, and no provision had been made for this eventuality. Canadian planners, in fact, had believed that most of the fighting equipment for Canadian troops would be provided from British stocks.

The generals were fully aware that thirty days training was worthless, and there is little doubt that their political superiors shared their view: Colonel J. Layton Ralston, the Minister of National Defence who had succeeded Norman Rogers after his death in an aircrash, was an infantry soldier from the Great War and a stickler for training. Ralston knew that four months training was the minimum necessary to produce even partially trained recruits, and the War Committee of cabinet confirmed this decision at the end of October. The attractions of using the conscripts for home defence, however, were very strong. Men who had volunteered for overseas service could be released from the defence of Canada and sent overseas if the draftees could be used to replace them. It was inevitable, therefore, that the term of service of the NRMA conscripts would be extended. At the end of April, 1941, it was announced that the first four months' trainees would be sent to coast defence units "thereby enabling the men in the coastal defence units in Canada to go overseas."[1] In all, 81,878 men had trained for the thirty-day period and been released.

THE VOLUNTARY SYSTEM ON TEST

Canada now had two armies: one for service anywhere in the world and one of conscripted men for service only in Canada. At first there was a strong group in the Department of National Defence who favoured segregating the training of the two groups, putting the conscripts off in little camps by themselves and treating them quite differently from the volunteers. After a fight, the decision was made to train the two classes of men together and to minimize the differences between them. In fact, this was the best method of seducing the conscripts into volunteering for overseas service. Many youths must have been frightened of the army, afraid that they were all thumbs or had two left feet. After a brief stint in the home defence force and after achieving some confidence, thousands decided to volunteer.

Many thousands of civilians, of course, enlisted voluntarily into the armed forces. Until the disasters of May and June, 1940 the flood of volunteers had been steady but not spectacular with 55,000 enlisting in September, 1939 and 2,000 to 6,000 each month thereafter. Enlistments after the fall of France were much higher, and by the end of 1941 there were 260,000 army volunteers for service anywhere in the world. The Royal Canadian Navy had increased tenfold since 1939, and its strength was over 20,000. The Royal Canadian Air Force, too, had found no shortage of volunteers, and it numbered close to 100,000 men by the end of 1941. In all, close to 400,000 men were under arms in Canada after 28 months of war, an astounding achievement and one that dwarfed the nation's contribution in the 1914 war. For a country with a population of only 11,500,000, simultaneously devoting every effort to increasing the production of food and of munitions, the number of volunteers was incredible.

But, as in the previous war, there was a strong feeling developing that Quebec was not doing its share. Arthur Meighen, for one, spent some time calculating just how far Quebec lagged behind Ontario in producing recruits, as one memorandum in his papers shows:[2]

Quebec population (1939 est.)   3,210,000   (Quebec is 85.5% of Ontario)

Ontario   3,752,000

As of October 31, 1941
    Ontario voluntary enlistments   147,114
    Quebec share (85.5%)   125,783
    Quebec actual   61,247

    Ontario overseas troops   89,618
    Quebec share (85.5%)   76,624
    Quebec actual   34,293

Superficially, Meighen's figures bolstered his argument that Quebec was not doing enough, that Quebec was uninterested in the war.

This attitude was unjust, however, as a very clear army report on "The Recruiting Problem in the Province of Quebec" pointed out. Such a view, the report noted, could be held only by those "who fail to appreciate either the tactless blunders of a past generation, or the difficult and complex obstacles to proportional mobilization of French-speaking army units."[3] Two problems were fundamental. The educational system in the Province of Quebec was based on metaphysics and not on physics, and so produced few men fitted for the technical services. Language was the second problem. Despite the lessons of the First World War, the Canadian armed forces remained unilingual. With one or two exceptions, all technical training manuals were available only in English. The language of instruction in all the engineering and specialist training centres was English. Officer training, too, was conducted only in one language.

To a French Canadian it must have seemed that every door but one—that leading to the infantry—was closed to him. The editor of the Montreal newspaper *Le Canada* told an Ontario audience:

> Even when joining the Army, French Canadians know that their chances for advancement are slight unless they are English-speaking. There is no French counterpart for Kingston Royal Military College . . . almost all the Canadian high command and superior staff officers are English speaking. . . .

There may have been good reasons for this, the journalist admitted, "but the fact nevertheless remains that in war as well as in peace, the French Canadian cannot escape the feeling that he is a second class citizen in his own country. . . ."[4]

Nonetheless, French Canadians had been enlisting in substantial numbers. Unfortunately, no official figures of the numbers of either French or English Canadians as such were kept in either of the two world wars, although estimates are available. One army report noted that on March 31, 1941 total army enlistments were 18 percent lower than on March 31, 1916, but Quebec enlistments were 15,000 men higher—58 percent higher —in 1941.[5] Another source calculated that in July 1943 there were 83,000 French-speaking or bilingual soldiers amounting to some 19 percent of army enlistments.[6] More French Canadians were enlisting, and there were any number of good reasons that could be advanced in explanation for those who refused to volunteer.

No such explanations could be acceptable to the increasing number of Canadians who began to press for conscription in the spring of 1941. The feeling of frustration was widespread throughout the country. Taxes were rising, sacrifices were being demanded, luxuries were disappearing from the market. The military situation continued to deteriorate in North Africa and in southeastern Europe, and there were still few Canadian casualties. If Canada had no casualties, how could she be doing her bit? One politician asked, "How many Germans have been killed by Canadian Forces?"[7] This query illustrates the emotional nature of the issue, the feeling that conscription was necessary to fight the war regardless of the effects it might have on national unity, regardless of the large air force and navy that had scarcely existed in the 1914 war, and regardless of the great strategic and tactical differences between the two world wars. Conscription was necessary, and there could be no argument about this if one were to be considered a true patriot, a true Canadian.

The demands for an end to the restrictions on the service of NRMA men began in the west. Murdoch MacPherson, a one-time Attorney-General of Saskatchewan and the runner-up to Dr. Manion at the Conservative leadership convention of 1938, was the first to speak out, despite a telegraphed warning from his party leader Hanson that he had better make it very clear that he was speaking on his own and not as a representative of the party. Others like Dr. Herbert Bruce, the former Lieutenant-Governor of Ontario and the M.P. for Toronto-Parkdale, soon followed. Dr. Bruce told the House of Commons in May, 1941:

> I am speaking only for myself when I call upon the government to take immediate steps to meet the present urgent situation and make available by a national selective process the men necessary to bring our armed forces up to the strength that represents the fighting might of Canada.[8]

Bruce and MacPherson, however, represented a minority of the Conservative party, or so at least thought Richard Hanson.

Writing to a correspondent who was insisting that Conservatives should lead in a fight for conscription, he said:

> From the very beginning of the war we have endeavoured to manoeuvre the position so that the Liberals will have to adopt conscription. Our view is that those who are anxious for conscription underestimate the sentiment in the country against it and that it is not opportune for us to come out at this time flatfooted for conscription.

The time will arrive, Hanson continued, and that time would be when the voluntary system had demonstrated its failure.

> Meanwhile our rural Members are absolutely opposed to it, and without unanimity in the Party here I could not take this step. My own view is in favour of conscription but I cannot carry the rank and file of the party in the House with me and it is useless to take this step without that unanimity. . . . You just have to balance things, one against the other.[9]

It seems clear that Hanson and his rural M.P.s remembered 1917.

Others, it seems, did not. And the opportunity to do something about their feelings was soon at hand. In May, 1941, the Conservative caucus had decided that a party meeting to select the date and site for a full-scale leadership convention should be held in November. But as Arthur Meighen wrote to a friend:

> I am steadily moving to the conviction that we ought to move faster than that and that the Conservative party has to take this thing in hand as its own mission, that it must choose its leader and choose him soon and get into action on strong British total war lines without delay. . . . I believe that whatever is done should be done this Fall.[10]

There was no mistaking the old leader's opinion.

Hanson was still standing by his belief that the time was not yet ripe for conscription, and a trip to the United Kingdom confirmed him in his position. Speaking to a gathering at Toronto's exclusively Conservative Albany Club on October 29, Hanson said:

> I have been urged to declare for conscription of manpower. What would happen if I did? Immediately the Conservative party in parliament nailed conscription to its masthead, we'd consolidate all those forces that have been opposed to us since 1917. . . . Conscription is bound to come to the front more and more insistently—but it must come from the people themselves. To make it a political move would defeat the very purpose of those who have it in view.[11]

Hanson's speech horrified the conscriptionists. Meighen wrote:

> Frankly his speech was a failure and has made a most unfortunate impression.[12]

The party meeting scheduled for November 7-8 gave those who favoured conscription their chance.

THE CONSERVATIVE POSITION CHANGES

The Conservative party conference that met in the Railway Committee rooms of the Parliament Buildings on November 7 had been called only for one purpose—to make arrangements for a leadership convention in 1942. But some Conservatives and some party newspapers—in particular the Toronto *Globe and Mail*—demanded that the meeting should not waste time and money and that it should take upon itself the task of selecting the new leader. What the party now required, the *Globe and Mail* stated, was "a man of ability with an established record and ample Parliamentary experience to serve as the spearhead of the Opposition forces in the House." These were difficult qualifications to fill in the tattered Conservative party of 1941, but the Toronto paper was equal to the task. The choice was revealed on November 4:

> . . . a leader of experience in war administration who is at the same time skilled in Parliamentary debate, equipped with a keen intellect and fortified by moral courage . . . Arthur Meighen.[13]

Very few could disagree with this assessment of Meighen. He was a parliamentary veteran, a skilled speaker, and a formidable intellect. But most agreed with another of the *Globe and Mail's* assessments:

> . . . all that has ever been said against him is that his political judgment is faulty.[14]

So it seemed to be. *Canadian Forum*, a left wing monthly that supported the CCF, hit the nail on the head when it wondered:

> . . . how any group of saviours-of-the-country, even with the *Globe and Mail* helping to pull the strings, could be so insane as to imagine that they have any chance of getting into power under the lead of the man whose record in the last war includes the alienation of the French by conscription, of the West by the War Times Election Act, and of labor by his activities in the Winnipeg strike. . . .[15]

These were formidable groups to have in opposition, but the backers of Meighen were more interested in his positive attributes. Here was the man who could put the fear of God into the Liberals—and particularly into Mackenzie King, for whom Meighen had utter contempt. Here was the man who could mobilize English Canada behind him and force the formation of a Union Government. Here was the man who could get conscription and put Canada's whole weight behind the Empire. And they were right. Meighen probably was the only man who stood a chance of doing these things.

As a result of the meeting Meighen was chosen leader. Curiously, Meighen himself was not completely easy in his mind about taking on the task of party leadership. He was sixty-seven years old, and his personal affairs were not in order, but how could he refuse?

> I became convinced, and certainly my wife became convinced, that I would lose what respect and regard the people felt for me if in the full light of day and with an appeal which had by that time reached Coast-to-Coast dimensions, I refused to try to do the one thing I can do, if, indeed, there is anything I can do, entirely well. . . .[16]

Meighen entered the lists against King immediately and released a long manifesto on November 13.

> A Government on a strictly party basis is in office and exercising despotic powers. This state of affairs in a war of life and death is anomalous. Such a Government cannot bring the whole nation to its maximum endeavour. . . . This nation is in the throes of crisis. . . . That Britain is doing its mightiest few will dispute. . . . Who will dare to say that Canada is even in sight of a total war? . . . I shall, therefore, urge with all the power I can bring to bear compulsory selective service over the whole field of war. . . .[17]

There could be no doubt about Meighen's policy. He was for conscription and national government. Mackenzie King would have to go. The policy in sum was to be 1917 all over again.

Mackenzie King, however, had no intention of accepting Meighen's interpretation of the political scene. He was definitely not amused by the return of his old antagonist, recording in his diary that, "life day by day will be made intolerable by his attacks, misrepresentations and the like." At a meeting of his cabinet on November 13, he pointed out:

> . . . my position now is the same as Sir Wilfrid's was in 1917: that Meighen was no longer for co-operation with Government policy, but opposition to Government policy —opposition first for conscription, National Government, and against our policies generally. It meant the financial forces and the press would rise against us.

But as King told his ministers, he would do nothing to block Meighen's entry into the House of Commons:

> While I saw Meighen's entry significant of strife, it was not for me to begin the strife by taking any step which could be construed as a desire to maintain government by party lines to the point of keeping out of the Commons the leader of another party. . . .[18]

The lines were clearly drawn for a slam-bang campaign on the issue of conscription, and the battleground would be the Toronto constituency of York South, selected by Meighen as the riding from which he would make his entry into the House of Commons. York South was a good riding for Meighen. It had been safely Conservative since its founding, and in 1940 it had returned a Conservative with a comfortable margin. And his chances were increased when the Liberals of York South announced that they would not run a candidate against Meighen. Only the Co-operative Commonwealth Federation would oppose the return to the House of Commons of the Tory chieftain.

Meighen fired his first shot in a radio address on January 9. His argument was simple but forceful:

> . . . we are not organized politically as we should be . . . we are not organzied militarily as we should be.

Even tiny New Zealand, Meighen claimed, had made a greater proportional effort than had Canada.

> We need more men for overseas service. We cannot organize this nation without ample power to direct the energies of every man and woman to the place where those energies are needed. That power this government refuses to exercise. The cold hand of political expediency has held it in its grip. A trembling servitude to a sinister tradition has gone far to benumb the striking power of Canada.

There could be no excuse for refusing to impose conscription in any war, Meighen continued. Certainly King's reason—"that if we compel Canadians to serve where Canadians have to fight to save Canada, we will destroy the unity of the Nation," as Meighen put it—was foolish.

> Can any normal mind accept such a preposterous contention?[19]

This was strong medicine Meighen was offering the voters.

The Right Honourable Arthur Meighen in a portrait used on his campaign literature for the York South by-election, February, 1942.

". . . a controversialist *par excellence* to whom conflict was the stuff of politics, he was a polarizing force ardently admired by his friends and bitterly disliked by many, though not all, of his opponents. He was a master of the spoken word to whom language was a weapon in a ceaseless argument, a weapon used to define issues and clarify differences rather than to emit platitudinous smokescreens."

Roger Graham, "Meighen in Debate", *Queen's Quarterly*, LII (Spring, 1955), p. 24.

So too was the formation of The Committee for Total War. By a "spontaneous and enthusiastic demonstration of the people's will" a committee had been formed at a meeting of approximately 200 substantial citizens in the Roof Garden of Toronto's Royal York Hotel.[20] The stated purpose of the Committee was to mobilize public opinion in support of conscription and to exert pressure on the Ontario Members of Parliament, hopefully forcing the Liberals among them to desert Prime Minister King. The formation of the Toronto 200, as the Committee came to be called, marked the shift of the conscription campaign into high gear. Meighen's election fight was merged into a province-wide struggle. Full page advertisements trumpeted the call for "Total War Now" in every daily and weekly newspaper in Ontario. Editorial writers pulled out all the stops as they demanded conscription now. In the *Globe and Mail*, the leader of the drive, the news columns began to read like the editorial pages and even the social pages had their message of conscription. As the *Globe and Mail* gleefully put it on January 13, "The heather is on fire in Ontario." So it was. The threat to the King government was a serious one.

Mackenzie King was convinced, however, that the demand for conscription in early 1942 was only a psychological one. There had been no difficulty in recruiting volunteers for overseas service. So far, there had been no casualties of sufficient number overseas to make reinforcements a problem. But King was a realist and a very practical politician. He knew that his opponents were trying to make conscription into the symbol of a total war effort, and he realized that his pledge not to conscript men could be an embarrassment when casualties eventually began to mount. As early as the middle of September, 1941 he had begun to search for ways around his promise, and the idea of a plebiscite was figuring more and more in his thinking.

A plebiscite—a vote on the question of conscription, but a vote that was in no way binding on the government—was the ideal way out of the box King could see being built around himself. With Meighen and the Toronto 200 all calling for conscription a plebiscite would outflank Meighen's attempt to win York South on a show of hands on the question of conscription. Only those who wanted conscription immediately, regardless of the situation in the country and regardless of national unity, would be compelled to vote for the Tory leader. Others could wait a month or two to express their opinion in a national ballot. Accordingly, the Speech from the Throne opening the 1942 session of parliament on January 22 included the following statement:

> My ministers . . . will seek, from the people, by means of a plebiscite, release from any obligation arising out of any past commitments restricting the methods of raising men for military service.[21]

Meighen's reaction to the plebiscite was to brand it as "political cowardice." Mitch Hepburn, the Ontario Liberal Premier, who was supporting Meighen in his by-election bid, swore that he would oppose the plebiscite to the end. "But I will go down with the flag to the mast and fighting for British principles."[22] Hypnotized by the issue of compulsory service, the conscriptionists believed that King's action would increase Meighen's chances for victory. Who could not be outraged by the government's lily-livered attempt to evade its responsibilities? But other observers noted that the plebiscite call had steadied the Grits behind their leader, and there now seemed to be no chance of the mass revolt the Toronto 200 had sought. In the public mind, attacks on the concept of the plebiscite seemed to be attacks on conscription itself. Of what was Meighen afraid, the public might well have asked? Whatever their disgust with King, the Conservatives had to work to bring out the largest possible vote on the plebiscite. They could not allow the idea of conscription to be defeated. Meighen's chief issue had been virtually destroyed; it is a measure of the man that he failed to realize this.

The CCF candidate running in York South against Arthur Meighen did not make the same mistake. Joseph Noseworthy was a school teacher at Vaughan Road Collegiate, located exactly in the middle of the constituency. As a local man, he knew that York South despite its long string of Conservative representatives was a special sort of constituency. Unemployment there had been dreadful during the depression. Most of the population was working class, and the successful Conservatives from the riding had always made a special effort to deal fairly with the needs of the workers. A campaign based on social welfare and pitched directly at the needs and fears of the ordinary people might be successful even against Arthur Meighen. This was Noseworthy's reasoning, and it proved to be correct.

Clearly, Noseworthy also benefited from a resentment on the part of some Liberals over the kind of campaign Meighen was running—attacking King and the Grits although they were not running a candidate against him. Professor Roger Graham, the able biographer of Meighen, has suggested that the Liberals actively campaigned for the CCF, motivated only by their desire to keep Meighen out of parliament.[23] There is some evidence of Liberal assistance to the CCF — at least $1,000 in Liberal funds was given to support the party campaign—but there is no sign of further assistance. Certainly old CCFers deny that the Liberals aided them. The election results, too, tend to support this argument. Meighen did very well in the usually Liberal areas of the riding. Where he lost, it is clear, is in the normally Tory working class districts where his support declined by 4,400 votes from that received by the victorious Conservative in the general election two years earlier. Meighen was defeated by working-class Conservatives. Conscription had been defeated by social welfare.

Mackenzie King was jubilant at the defeat of his old antagonist. One story has it that he called up the leader of the CCF, M. J. Coldwell, and told him that if titles were given in Canada he would have made him a Knight Commander of the Bath. In his diary, he jubilantly noted Meighen's defeat:

> . . . in the strongest riding in Toronto, which means the strongest Tory riding in all of Canada. Defeated, while supported by financial interests and the press—everything in the way of organization and campaign power that could be assembled for any man. . . .[24]

The major effect of the York South by-election was to take the steam out of the Conservative party's drive for conscription and national government. The Conservatives were left with their big issue in ruins. King's shrewd expedient of the plebiscite had mouse-trapped Arthur Meighen. The real gainers from the Noseworthy victory, however, were the CCF. For the first time, they received national attention, and from this point they never looked back. The party soon established itself as a major contender for power, and by 1943 the CCF led the Liberals and Conservatives in the Gallup polls. This lead was short-lived, but the CCF had arrived as a major party after York South.

THE PLEBISCITE

The question of the plebiscite remained to be answered. How would the country vote? Meighen's defeat seemed to indicate that English Canadians were not entirely convinced conscription was immediately necessary. Reports by political observers from rural areas confirmed this point of view. British Columbia, its Pacific Coast exposed to Japanese attack, was apparently revising its early sentiments in favour of conscription. Now, the press reports had it, British Columbia wanted the boys kept home. The question was very much in doubt.

But clearly King wanted release from his early promises against conscription. A free hand would give him the greatest possible manoeuverability. The question that would be on the ballots for the April 27 plebiscite, therefore, had to be framed very carefully. The result was a masterpiece of political ambiguity:

> Are you in favour of releasing the Government from any obligations arising out of any past commitments restricting the methods of raising men for military service?

The word conscription had been carefully left off the ballot.

And clearly King had put the opposition in an uncomfortable position. How could they oppose him on this issue? The Members could denounce the Prime Minister for the greatest "lack of national leadership this country has ever witnessed,"[25] but still the dilemma stared them in the face. The perplexed and troubled R. B. Hanson wrote to his nephew overseas:

> I have been giving some thought as to how I should vote personally. If I vote "No" I am in effect telling King that he has been right all along and that he should adhere to his policy of "no conscription for overseas service". . . . If I vote "Yes" and to relieve him of his obligations, I have not the slightest assurance in the world that he will do anything. . . .[26]

Yet as every Conservative was aware, they could not afford to see conscription beaten, and eventually even Arthur Meighen indicated that he would support the government's campaign to be freed of its pledges. Mackenzie King had manoeuvered his opponents into working for his policy.

An advertisement placed by an all-party committee in the
Toronto *Globe and Mail*, 24 April 1942.

The problem of Quebec, however, was still there. King after
all had made his pledges against conscription directly and
explicitly to Quebec. Now he was asking all Canada to release

him from his promises. How would Quebec react to this move?

The response was not long in coming. In the House of Commons, Maxime Raymond, an independently-minded and *nationaliste* Quebec M.P., stated the issue as he saw it:

> We are not separatists, but let us not be forced to become separatists. We wish indeed to dwell in the same house, but the house must be habitable for all. We are partisans of national unity, but according to certain equitable conditions, and when our conditions have been fixed in advance, we ask that they be observed.

Then Raymond continued with a look at the conscription sentiment in Toronto:

> And I fear that the "Two Hundred" of Toronto, who agitate in favour of conscription for service overseas in violation of the pact of September 1939, are about to forge the nails which will serve to seal the coffin of national unity, and perhaps of Confederation.[27]

Within a few weeks, *La Ligue Pour La Défense du Canada* was formed. Its object was to mobilize the greatest possible vote against releasing King from his promises. Why should you vote "No"? the manifesto of the *Ligue* asked Quebeckers:

> Because no one asks to be relieved of a pledge unless he is already planning to violate it, and because of all the promises made to the people of Canada there is none that King is more obliged to keep: the promise not to conscript men for overseas.[28]

The *Ligue* was on solid ground in its complaints against the plebiscite concept.

Curiously, in the light of this opposition to a "Yes" vote, the government ran an incredibly feeble campaign. Certainly there were some speakers in Quebec who called for a "Yes" vote, and the clergy seemed to be adopting an attitude of benevolent neutrality. But for every Liberal M.P. who urged his people to vote "Yes", a dozen stood silent or urged their people to vote

INDEX
Amusements—16   Serial—17
Births, Deaths—16   Social—22-23
Comics—21-22   Sports—
Markets—14-15   Women's—
Radio—19   Women's—20-21

TORONTO DAILY STAR

50TH YEAR

TORONTO, TUESDAY, APRIL 28, 1942—34 PAGES

THE WEATHER
City and lower lakes—Wednesday
Fair and warm with strong winds.
Low weight, 36; high tomorrow, 58.

3c PER COPY, 18c PER WEEK

RAIDERS, MILE SQUARE, HIT NAZI

Forecast Conscription After 'Smashing Yes'

BURMA CRISIS NEAR, JAP FLEET SIGHTED

BOMBERS SWARM AGAIN FROM DAWN TO DAWN UNCHALLENGED BY FOE

Thirty Nazi Fighters Veer Out of Path of R.A.F. to Avoid Combat—Airdromes, Docks, Ships Are Blasted

TODAY'S ATTACKING UNIT AT CALAIS COVERS MILE OF SKY, LONDON SAYS

London, April 28—British bombers, continuing massed raids against German targets, last night attacked Cologne and other Rhineland objectives. The naval base at Trondheim, the docks at Dunkirk and airdromes in German-occupied territory also were bombed, an air ministry communique announced today. Eighteen planes were lost.

A new bomber unit fighting attacking force covering a square mile of sky and described as "the largest single unit ever to attack occupied France" swept out towards Calais today. Smaller flights had already returned from earlier raids which began at dawn.

In the night raids, as R.A.F. bombers raided Germany and Trondheim, coastal command planes damaged a German supply ship off the Danish coast and fighter command planes attacked airdromes in occupied territory.

Eastwick In Ruins

Dispatches from Stockholm revealed, on the basis of reports direct from Berlin, that in four nights of pulverizing raids Britain's bombers had left Rostock, great Baltic port and seat of the Heinkel plane works, a city of smouldering ruins, and said that after tons of thousands had wandered homeless about its ruined streets for days the German was now evacuating almost the entire population. Special trains and buses were requisitioned to effect the evacuation, the dispatches said.

German sources were quoted as admitting also that British planes had dropped leaflets over Rostock, 45 miles east of Rostock, warning townspeople that the R.A.F. was going to bomb it on the next visit to the Baltic shores.

10th Raid on Cologne

The air ministry, in its summonique on the night raids, said great lives were left burning at Cologne and other targets in the Rhineland.

But it added that the effect of the raid on Trondheim, where the Germans have been strongholds fortifying for months to fear of a British invasion attack, might not be known for some time.

Instead of antiaircraft ten foot

LOST ARM IN '41 TODAY FLIES AGAIN SHOOTS DOWN FOE

London, April 28—(CP)— Squadron Leader J. A. F. MacLachlan, the R.A.F.'s one-armed D.F.C.-and-bar fighter pilot, shot down his first enemy plane today since he was equipped with artificial arm specially devised for handling Hurricane controls. MacLachlan's left arm was amputated above the elbow after he was wounded by a Messerschmitt cannon shell over Malta in March, 1941. Prior to the amputation he had a record bag of 13 German and Italian aircraft.

MAY KNOW TODAY IF CANADA TO BREAK TIES WITH VICHY

May Ask for Recall of Minister Here—Silent on Report of Break

REVIEW RELATIONS

Ottawa, April 28—(CP)—Prime Minister King is scheduled to make a statement in the House of Commons today on relations between Canada and Vichy France. Possibly the statement would have to be postponed for the credentials of the French minister here, René Ristelhueber.

Neither Mr. King nor his senior officers in the external affairs department would comment on a report that Canada is contemplating calling off diplomatic relations with Vichy France.

When France and became virtual head of the French government a fortnight ago, Mr. King said the whole question of French relations would have to be re-examined in view of Laval's pro-Axis attitude.

He added yesterday that he would ask his officers to make a statement today. Mr. King added that it was a question of external affairs and would have to be considered in Canada's future relations with France in view of the recent formation of Laval's cabinet. He said British attitude should be broken with Vichy, but that Britain had been broken with Vichy, and Canada might follow.

He said that he would be prepared to make a statement today. Mr. King added that it was a question as to whether regrettable matter he would intimate to any who would. Mr. King said Canada had been associated the partnership question.

France had had a minister in Ottawa for nearly 50 years and the present minister came in the capital.

JAPS MOVE FAST FLANK MANDALAY IN 93-MILE PUSH

AVG Fliers Down Eleven Planes From Fleet of Fifty

3-PRONGED DRIVE

Chungking, April 28—(BUP)— Japanese mechanized columns, bypassing Mandalay in a flanking movement, threatened today in the Burma front thrust at Lashio, threatening the entire Burma-Chinese defence system in eastern Burma's Shan states.

London reported Japanese shipping was sighted in the Bay of Bengal by Allied reconnaissance planes. The ships were believed moving as reinforcements to Burma.

American "Flying Tiger" pilots today shot down at least 11 of a fleet of about 50 Japanese planes that bombed their northern Burma base and set fire to Lashio. The U.S. fliers escaped without a single loss.

The Japanese planes were blasting and setting fire to scores of towns and villages and terrorizing native populations in their wide-spread attacks.

(Competent London observers feared that the war along the Burma-Chinese border may end the fate of Burma within the next few days. They pointed out that Japanese capture of the Mandalay-Lashio railway would cut off the last "reasonably easy" route of escape for the main British-Chinese forces in eastern and central Burma.

Late dispatches from Chungking said 100,000 Japanese troops were attacking in northeastern Burma and that the situation was in grave the Chinese had started systematic destruction of roads leading to Lashio in an effort to delay enemy motorized columns.

A Chinese communique tonight said enemy spearheads within 40 miles of Lashio admitted the British and Chinese defenders faced the gravest threat of the Burma campaign.

The Japanese clearly intended striking first at Lashio, to cut off the main supply and communications route to China. The enemy column, which drove directly north from Lashio has reached a point northwest of Mandalay, and Chinese headquarters said the battle for Lashio may be fought before the battle for Mandalay.

A communique placed the Japanese spearhead near Kyaukse, 30 miles north of Thazi. The other was said to have reached Mong Kung, 40 miles east of Kengtung bypassing and only 87 miles from Lashio.

Almost straight east of Lashio, another Japanese column was reported to have reached Kengtung, 75-mile advance. This unit apparently was attempting to reach Chinese forces still fighting in the southern Shan states along the Thai frontier and prevent them from joining troops in the north in defence of the Burma Road.

F.D.R. AT 10 TONIGHT ON CFRB AND CKCL

Toronto radio stations, CFRB and CKCL, will carry President Roosevelt's speech tonight when he goes on the air at 10 o'clock. The speech is scheduled to last half an hour. Mr. Roosevelt will explain to the nation his seven-point "equality of privilege" program to hold down the cost of living, which he is expected to recapture yesterday. His talk is being broadcast by networks and will also be sent via short-wave all over the world.

(a) just before the fall of France in the spring of 1940.

Mr. King held parliament that the recent on general assurance that the British government wished relations to be maintained between Canada and Vichy. Although Britain had broken relations with Vichy, France broke off relations with Britain.

BERNE SAYS GIRAUD IS OUT OF GERMANY

Swiss Say Escaped General Has Moved On

London, April 28—(CP)—Reuters said today in a Berne dispatch that Gen. Henri Giraud, French commander in the "Battle of the Bulge," has escaped through the German lines of detained April 21 after escape from the German fortress of Koenigstein, where it was a prisoner of war. The Nazis have offered 100,000 marks to for recapture.

Reuters said Gen. Giraud had not been captured so far Saturday but on

THE COMMANDER-IN-CHIEF SIGNS UP
President Franklin Delano Roosevelt, commander-in-chief of the 18,000,000 citizens in the U.S. age group who registered yesterday in the selective service manpower inventory. James D. Jaffess.

GALLUP POLL RIGHT TO 4 P.C. TOLD VOTE 2 DAYS BEFORE

Public Opinion Institute Scores Success in First Big Canadian Test

By the Canadian Institute of Public Opinion

Faced with one of the severest tests possible in such an examination, the Canadian Institute of Public Opinion (Gallup Poll) proved the almost uncanny accuracy of its methods in the Dominion. It predicted the outcome of the national manpower plebiscite, not only to forecasting with 100 per cent accuracy which provinces would vote yes and which no, but also by predicting the actual percentage majorities in each province within an average of four than five per cent. The national vote was forecast within about four per cent.

In other words, through the medium of this wide closely constructed device for measured what the public is thinking, readers of the newspaper knew on Saturday just what the public thought for the Canadian public were going to vote on Monday.

These returns are not complete, and individuals not the reports of water may actually be reduced in some provinces and in the national total.

Here is the record. It is based on early returns (up to 9 a.m. on Tuesday) and shows the percentages published in these columns on Saturday, followed by actual broken off relations with Britain.

	Gallup	Actual
Province	Yes	Yes

STUDENT RIOTS SHUT ATHENS UNIVERSITY

London, April 28—(CP)—Greek government sources here said today the University of Athens had been closed for an indefinite period because of serious student disturbances.

FUEHRER FIRES NAZI GENERAL ON FINN FRONT

Russians Win Control of Entire Region Around Lake Ilmen

NAZIS OUTFLANKED

London, April 28—The Russians appeared to have won control of the entire region around Lake Ilmen today, except for German pockets in Novgorod and Staraya Russa by an outflanking movement.

Adolf Hitler today fired the entire German high command, and took over direct command of the armies himself, from which he was expecting favor, and was reliably reported replaced the commander-in-chief of the German forces on the Finnish front.

Military experts here said the situation fronts for the German general both north and south of the big lake, 130 miles below Leningrad. They said German communication to the rear also were threatened.

GIVEN A DECISIVE 'YES' MR. KING SAYS 'WILL OF MAJORITY PREVAILS'

Atlantic to Pacific, Every Province Except Quebec in the Affirmative

"GET ON WITH IT"

By H. E. ARMSTRONG

Ottawa, April 28—Early, though perhaps not immediate, adoption of conscription for overseas service is forecast here today following yesterday's tremendous affirmative majority on the plebiscite.

It is expected that a conscription act will be introduced in parliament either in June or July, before it adjourns, or in the fall when it meets again.

By a majority of more than 1,300,000 the Canadian people yesterday freed the hands of the King government.

Every province but Quebec voted overwhelmingly to release the government from its "no overseas conscription" pledge. In the largest vote in its history, Quebec declared itself as decisively in favor of holding the administration to its non-conscript overseas commitment—overseas conscription.

In the light of the tremendous affirmative majority and in the light of the distinct cleavage between English-speaking and French-speaking opinion, Premier King has no doubt that his government will inaugurate overseas conscription if...

Will of Majority Prevails

"There can be no doubt as to the significance of the vote," this prime minister declared in a statement issued shortly after midnight. "It will be interpreted throughout the country that the will of the majority prevails.

Declaring the large affirmative vote has "freed the hands of the government, Mr. King said that it will not be construed as a vote of confidence in the government up to now or any particular party.

Hon. J. L. Ralston, minister of national defence, was equally emphatic in interpreting the conscription balloting. "I am pleased beyond the usual bounds," he said.

92 IN 100 VOTED 'YES' IN TORONTO

Ninety-two per cent of Toronto's voters marked their ballots "yes" in the plebiscite. Toronto's total for cities follows:

	Yes	No
Toronto	207,607	21,215
Ottawa	40,588	13,503
Hamilton	65,420	6,127
Montreal	282,951	245,665
Winnipeg	110,584	15,260
Calgary	30,145	5,116
Vancouver	112,088	26,416

It will be a record vote for the Dominion.

Though the split between French-speaking and English-speaking sections of the country was marked in yesterday's voting, it was not so wide as in 1917, in the wartime election on conscription.

Yesterday, as for Quebec voting all in Montreal, the total affirmative vote on the plebiscite in question and the whole city of Montreal had only a bare majority against releasing the government from its commitment on overseas conscription. In the 1917 federal conscription, municipalities, most of them large French-speaking, elected anti-conscription candidates in earlier day's voting only four Outer ridings, Russell and Prescott, gave negative answer. This despite the fact that the French-speaking vote is considerable to at least 40 municipalities in the province.

The possibility of the other provinces giving a large affirmative vote and Quebec a decisive negative pronouncement has been continued in government circles for some time the possible solution, to ask Quebec to accept the Dominion-wide decision—and overseas conscription, if necessary. If it needed it seems, a solution that the government was striving for to save national unity.

'No' in Minority' Ridings

It is evident that several able ministers and many members advocated an affirmative answer. French-speaking ridings that political debate. The Quebec minorities represented by Mr. G. Power, Sen. Louis St. Leo and Hon. P. J. A. Cardin, and New Brunswick riding of Hon. Michaud all rolled up substantial negative majorities.

In the view that Quebec as permitted to fall in line with other provinces now that the plebiscite has been pronounced. it has driven, the government is encouraged by the vote of districts that are since yesterday no at times with a sizeable trouble during 1917 conscription crisis.

Though the differences of opinion on a sharp feeling does not show as high as in 1917, The war spirit is also more across for Canada than it was then, and there is clearly more signs of action on Canadian soil.

The admitted need of higher defence over Nazi aggression. heavy rolling over Canada-wide the course of the government. It is possible that, when the active service balloting results are known, as May's first dead result will be seen to find as near to overwhelming. In every section of the Dominion as the balloting is now known.

With nearly 550,000 more than 1,000 German soldiers destroyed and less than part and many mechanized may add ask be 4,686,422 polled to the number of yes. In excess, any instance of the Dominion.

Aussies Even Want to Send Their Home Militia to Atta

Melbourne, April 28—(AAP)—the militia, which is now in the a of all other respects and on in fighting on the Australia of Fiji Darwin. Eastern Australia of Fiji Darwin. Eastern Australia to "If wanted be unlimited war on the place the Australian government or adequate opposed. prevails cabinet, many party conscription supporter push a contingent part of the Pacific war. The militia war cannot be were a "Australia now would be part of reinforcement of Australia.

The Pacific war cannot be won until the offensive over the Japanese the full command and equipment seems abandoned. "Australia should raise by compulsory drafting about tons a party Japanese offensive. If effective the present government is maintained and men of Australia's effort.

The Australian Imperial reinforcement now being built up to overseas service may if over the position in Australia of the Pacific war.

How Provinces Voted On Plebiscite Shown

Canadian Press plebiscite vote tabulated by provinces at noon today (with percentages bracketed):

Province	Yes	No	Polls Reported
P.E.I. (80)	21,423	4,360	239 of 241
Nova Scotia (77)	116,753	35,799	1,624 of 1,694
New Brunswick (70)	102,017	43,340	970 of 1,179
Quebec (28)	372,666	942,110	7,113 of 7,974
Ontario (84)	1,100,500	229,311	10,150 of 10,565
Manitoba (80)	217,299	48,800	1,640 of 1,845
Saskatchewan (71)	175,969	61,863	7,040 of 7,201
Alberta (70)	169,619	63,523	2,084 of 2,551
British Columbia (80)	247,987	...842	2,194 of 2,320
Yukon (88)	2,789	259	3 of 10
Totals (64)	2,612,963	1,486,771	39,625 of 31,568

THE WEATHER

"No". For example, the Liberal constituency organization in Dorchester-Bellechasse published a newspaper calling upon the voters to "Go to the Polls by Car or on Foot. Vote No." Ernest Lapointe, dead since November, 1941, was quoted in his promises to the province that there would never be conscription. *"Votons Non."*[29] And no public money could be spent to encourage a "Yes" vote, the government taking the position that it would have to provide equal funds to the other side and that this would not be in the public interest.

The results were striking. English Canadians voted overwhelmingly in favour of releasing the government from its past promises: Ontario by 82.3 percent; Prince Edward Island by 82.4 percent; British Columbia by 79.4 percent; and the rest by substantial margins. In Quebec, however, only 27 percent of the electorate voted "Yes". Quebec stood alone in insisting that the pledges made to it should be kept. Mackenzie King's problem now was to act in such a way that he could satisfy English Canadians who not unreasonably looked on the results as guaranteeing the implementation of conscription and at the same time not wholly alienate Quebec. The task was only slightly less difficult than squaring the circle.

King began by introducing on May 11 House of Commons Bill No. 80 to amend the National Resources Mobilization Act and repeal its limiting clause prohibiting the employment of conscripts overseas. Despite King's explanation that the amendment did not denote any change in government policy—an extraordinary statement from any point of view — P. J. A. Cardin, the senior French-Canadian minister since Lapointe's death, resigned. Cardin must have known, however, that King had no intention of proceeding with conscription for the foreseeable future, and his departure did nothing more than to strengthen the hand of the conscriptionists in the cabinet. As a result, for the next two months King was in a delicate position, tiptoeing first this way in an effort to restrain his English-speaking ministers, tiptoeing next that way to mollify the Canadiens.

His solution announced on June 10 was a masterful piece of

◀ The front page of the *Toronto Daily Star* for 28 April 1942.

political tactics. To satisfy Quebec, he emphasized that conscription was not yet necessary, might never be necessary, and would only be resorted to as a last resort. His phrasing of the policy has since become famous:

Not necessarily conscription, but conscription if necessary.[30]

At the same time, to satisfy Ontario and the conscriptionists, King agreed that the merits of conscription would not be debated in parliament again. Should it be necessary to impose conscription, King said, he would proceed by Order-in-Council, coming to the House of Commons only for a vote of confidence on whether or not his government should stay in power. King's delicate treading along the lines had produced the only possible policy. The circle had been squared, and the government's Bill No. 80 passed.

*   *   *

Conscription for overseas service was now the law of the land. King was obviously banking on the fact that he would never have to implement it, but the power was there. Perhaps the most important result of the crisis was that French Canada felt itself betrayed. Even Mackenzie King, the heir of Laurier, had let the *Québecois* down. After this no federal leader would ever be regarded with total confidence by French Canada. The crisis of 1942 was the turning point for Quebec. Now the French Canadians believed that it was only a matter of time before the conscriptionists of English Canada would have their way. Conscription was sure to come.

Chapter IV

The Second Conscription Crisis: 1944

Mackenzie King had managed to get through the conscription crisis of 1942 with a whole skin. The Conservatives were in disarray after Meighen's drubbing in York South. The cabinet, except for Cardin, had held together. There were severe grumblings from Quebec to be sure, but after all no conscription had yet been necessary. The Prime Minister was certain that it would never be necessary.

The course of the war seemed to be bearing out King's optimism. Late in 1942 the tide began to turn against the Nazis and the Japanese. The Russians had stopped the *Wehrmacht* at Stalingrad on the Volga and had inflicted a horrendous defeat on German arms. In North Africa, General Montgomery had defeated Rommel's *panzers* at El Alamein, and the Americans under Eisenhower had landed in Morocco and Algeria. In the Pacific theatre, the Japanese had rolled through the Philippine Islands, the Dutch East Indies, Malaya, and Hong Kong, but the United States Navy had destroyed substantial elements of the Imperial fleet at the battle of the Coral Sea. Victory over the Axis powers was now a possibility.

CANADIANS OVERSEAS

For Canada, the war was still relatively far away. Canadian troops had not participated in any of the North African fighting, and the Canadian Corps was still situated in England, defending the British Isles. There had been one or two occasions when the British High Command wanted to employ Canadian soldiers abroad piecemeal, but the Corps Commander, General Andrew McNaughton, was adamant that the Corps be employed as a corps. The reasoning was simple and probably correct: the only way that the Canadian government could control the fate and fortunes of its men was if they were kept together.

The government had one horrible example of what might occur if this principle was neglected. Approximately 2,000 Canadians had been lost when the Crown Colony of Hong Kong fell to the Japanese on Christmas Day, 1941. The troops, soldiers of the Winnipeg Grenadiers and the Royal Rifles of Canada, had been sent to the tiny colony off the Chinese coast at the direct request of the British government. Two battalions of infantry, Canada was told, would improve the defences of the island and perhaps act as a deterrent to the ambitious expansionism of Japan. The British intelligence estimates, of course, turned out to have scant basis in fact. Hong Kong was attacked on December 8, 1941, the day after Pearl Harbour, and the colony fell easily to the Japanese. The entire Canadian contingent was killed or captured to a man.

The Hong Kong disaster was thrown into the political arena in Canada early in 1942 by George Drew, the Conservative party leader in Ontario. Drew charged that untrained men had been sent to the Pacific, and he claimed that this showed how desperate the government was for military manpower. The implication was that conscription was necessary. Drew and other critics were also very harsh on the government for sending troops without sufficient support halfway across the world when war in the Pacific was imminent, and they claimed that much of the equipment for the force had never reached Hong Kong.

These were serious charges, and the King government appointed a Royal Commission under the Chief Justice of Canada, Sir Lyman Duff, to investigate. The Duff Commission's report has been characterized as a "whitewash", but in fact its findings were the only ones possible under the circumstances. Yes, the Chief Justice concluded, some relatively untrained men had been sent with the battalions; yes, the transport vehicles for the force had been shipped on a separate ship after the force had departed for Hong Kong; and yes, the vehicles had never reached the island. But, as noted, there was no expectation that war would occur in the Pacific as soon as it did. The Americans and the Japanese, after all, were conducting negotiations in Washington. And the Chief Justice concluded that the relatively few men whose training was incomplete did little to affect the fighting efficiency of the infantry.

The key point at issue, however, was not one on which the Royal Commission could properly comment. Drew and his cohorts objected to Canada's sending forces to Hong Kong. But what would have happened if the government had refused the British request? Canada then would have been letting down the Empire. The government then would have been attacked for not having enough troops because of the voluntary recruiting system to send men to Hong Kong. The Liberal government clearly was damned if it did and damned if it did not.

If there was any real lesson that had been learned by the Hong Kong fiasco, it was that Canada needed its own sources of foreign, political and military intelligence. The Canadian government had been led down the garden path by its willingness to accept British assessments of the situation.

There was to be yet another disaster to Canadian arms in 1942: Dieppe. From a force of 5,000 men who fought on the beach at Dieppe for only some nine hours, the Canadian army lost 3,367 casualties. The two brigades from the 2nd Canadian Division had been sent on a "reconnaissance in force" to test the feasibility of taking a port by direct assault. They learned that it was not feasible. The Germans, well-situated on the heights above the beaches, poured deadly fire into the soldiers struggling to get through the sand to cover. In virtually every respect the operation was a shambles.

Fortunately, Dieppe was the last calamity to befall the Canadian army. In 1943 the 1st Canadian Division (separated from the Canadian Corps in England over General McNaughton's objections) took part in the invasion of Sicily and the subsequent attack on Italy. It was joined by additional Canadian troops there, and soon there was a second Canadian Corps. At last Canadian forces were participating as full-fledged formations in the Second World War.

DOMESTIC POLITICS

Politically, the latter half of 1942 and all of 1943 were quiet in Canada. The Liberals continued to control the situation to their satisfaction (if that of few others). The conscription crisis of 1942 seemed forgotten after the plebiscite and Bill 80, and Mackenzie King showed no signs of willingness to use his power to send NRMA soldiers overseas.

But there were signs of restlessness among the electorate. The Co-operative Commonwealth Federation was increasing its strength, riding the crest of its upset defeat of Arthur Meighen in York South. And certainly the CCF had much in its favour. People were tired of the war, tired of high taxes, afraid for the future. A whole generation that knew nothing but depression and war had grown up, and it wanted a guarantee for the future. The CCF seemed to provide this. Social welfare for everyone was what the CCF promised. Government planning, CCF spokesmen said, would ensure jobs for all. In support of this claim, the CCF pointed to the booming factories of wartime Canada. This, they said, was accomplished through planning; the same thing could be done after the war. The result of the CCF drive was an enormous gain in support for the party until, in September, 1943, the Canadian Institute of Public Opinion reported that the socialists led the Liberals and Conservatives in popular support.

For the Conservative opposition, these figures were terrifying. Somehow the Conservative party had to be refurbished, rearmed with new policies and new ideas. The trend was already under way. After Meighen's defeat in York South, some progressive Conservatives began to realize that the party needed some policy other than conscription if it was to survive. The policy they hit upon was calculated to steal the thunder of the CCF: social welfare.

The resulting Conservative conference that met at Port Hope, Ontario in September, 1942 turned the Tory party toward social welfare. Conscription, too, was kept as a part of the party's policy, but it seemed clear that social welfare was more important. The Port Hope policies were transformed into official party dogma at the Conservative leadership convention at Winnipeg in December, 1942. There the party selected as its new chief the Liberal-Progressive Premier of Manitoba, John Bracken, and at his request the party's name was changed to

Progressive Conservative. Bracken had no previous connection with Conservatism, but he had a reputation as a moderate, pragmatic reformer. This was enough for the party progressives. Curiously, however, Bracken was also the choice of the conscriptionists who saw the Manitoban as an opponent of King's temporizing policies. Significantly, however, the Conservative party platform produced by the convention did not so much as mention the word conscription.

Clearly, the political parties were gearing up to fight the postwar election. And clearly the issue that they were preparing to fight about was social welfare. But Mackenzie King, by virtue of being in power, had certain advantages that the CCF and the Conservatives lacked. He could implement social welfare measures now. The result was the "baby bonus" legislation that was passed into law in 1944. A payment of approximately five dollars per month would be made to the mother of every child in the land. Estimates for the cost of this scheme were $250,-000,000—an amount that was almost half of the federal government's total expenditure before the outbreak of war. This was social welfare legislation. Mackenzie King had gone a long way toward regaining the upper hand for the Liberal party. The only thing that could block his return to office was another set-to over conscription.

CONSCRIPTION IS RAISED AGAIN

Conscription—the cursed subject was once again entering the newspapers in 1944. The reasons at first were primarily political. On June 15, 1944, the province of Saskatchewan elected the first socialist government in North America, returning the CCF under T. C. Douglas with a sweeping majority. To both Conservatives and Liberals this was an unnerving experience. Saskatchewan was the home province of Jimmy Gardiner, the Liberal Minister of Agriculture and a political boss in the old style. Now even this political fief was lost to the CCF. For the Tories, too, the Douglas win was a setback. Conservative leader Bracken's prairie reputation had been expected to help the provincial party, but it had not. The Conservative candidate in every single riding had run third; each had lost his deposit for not polling at least half as many votes as the winner.

The Tory failure in Saskatchewan ended the party's brief flirtation with social welfare. Welfare policies had had no effect in Saskatchewan, reasoned the party old guard, so they would have to go. But what could replace them? What issue could be used to sweep the Conservative party into power? What better issue could there be than conscription?

The times were more in the Conservative party's favour than they had been in 1942. Now Canadian troops were fighting, and now the soldiers were taking heavy casualties. The Normandy invasion on June 6, 1944 had opened up the second front at last, and if the end of the war could now be foreseen, there was certain to be much bloodshed before victory was achieved.

Just four days after the total Tory defeat in Saskatchewan, the issue of conscription once more came to the fore. The scene was Guelph, Ontario where Hon. C. P. McTague, who had been the chairman of the National War Labour Board and a justice of the Ontario Supreme Court until his resignation from these positions to become National Chairman of the Progressive Conservative Party, was addressing his own nomination meeting. With John Bracken, the party leader, sitting beside him, McTague laid it right on the line:

> Now as to where this party stands on this matter, let me state in simple unequivocal terms. To our army overseas and their relatives here we say you should have reinforcements now, and they are all available now, from the trained troops not now and never required for home defence. . . . National honour demands that without an hour's delay the necessary order in council should be passed making these reinforcements available. . . .

And if anyone had still missed the point, McTague continued:

> The government's persistence in leaving these trained soldiers of the home army in Canada, can only be construed as deference to the will of the minority in the Province of Quebec as voiced in the plebiscite. . . .[1]

There is some question as to whether or not Bracken knew what his lieutenant was going to say, but he could scarcely let McTague's remarks pass unnoticed:

> In this time of national emergency, surely there will be no Canadians who will find it in their heart to deny that appeal. Certainly it receives the endorsement of this party. . . .[2]

For the Conservative Members of Parliament, however, conscription still posed few attractions. The caucus was up in arms at the statements of both McTague and Bracken, statements that had been made without consultation. As a result, when an attempt was made on July 24, 1944 to have the party bring conscription to a vote in the House of Commons, the caucus flatly refused. Rodney Adamson, the M.P. for York West, wrote in his diary: "Caucus is 100% against taking this suicidal step. Really a great show and a sock in the eye for the Toronto crowd."[3] The Toronto crowd Adamson referred to consisted of such men as McTague, George Drew, by now the Conservative premier of Ontario, and George McCullagh, the publisher of the Toronto *Globe and Mail*. All these men felt as had Meighen two years earlier—Canada could not be doing her share in the war unless conscription for overseas service was enforced.

The curious thing was that as late as August, 1944 there was absolutely no shortage of infantry reinforcements for the frontlines. On August 3, the Chief of Staff of Canadian Military Headquarters in London, General Kenneth Stuart, had reported to the cabinet that while the army had been fighting twelve months in Italy and two months in France, the "reinforcement situation [was] very satisfactory. There were," he said, "reinforcement personnel available for three months at intensive battle casualty rate."[4]

But by the early fall, there were definitely shortages of trained infantry. What had gone wrong? The fault, it is clear, did not lie with the politicians but with the generals. The Canadian Army had adopted the British army's casualty estimating system as its guide for the training of reinforcements. The British had guessed that 48 percent of casualties would be infantrymen, but in fact 75 percent were. The German Air Force was now too weak to strafe the rear areas, and as a result there were few casualties among the supporting troops. Huge surpluses of men began to build up in the supply corps, and it became necessary to "convert" these men into infantry. Unfortunately, all too often the conversion training was perfunctory, and men were thrown into action without proper training. News of this state of affairs reached the Canadian public when Major Connie Smythe, the owner of hockey's Toronto Maple Leafs who had been commanding an anti-aircraft battery in Normandy, charged on his return home in September that some infantry reinforcements had "never thrown a grenade."[5]

The Minister of National Defence, Colonel Ralston, was preparing for his annual trip overseas when the Smythe story broke in the press. His investigations confirmed the situation, and

The Honourable J. L. Ralston, Minister of National Defence, inspecting Canadian troops, October 1941.

"Honest, forthright, sincere, his qualities had won the admiration and high regard of all with whom he came in contact. . . . When he thought of the army he thought of the private who had told him of his troubles a few weeks before, of the wounded he had talked to in the hospitals, of the courage, *esprit de corps*, and other fine characteristics which he knew from experience were evoked by exposure to common dangers on the battlefield."

R. MacGregor Dawson, *The Conscription Crisis of 1944* (Toronto: University of Toronto Press, 1961), p. 29.

the Minister had to be told by his generals that there had been a miscalculation: 15,000 additional trained infantry would have to be sent from Canada before the new year to meet the estimated demands in Northwest Europe and Italy. Thoroughly disillusioned by the conditions he had seen overseas, Ralston returned to Ottawa on October 18. He was ready to demand that the 15,000 reinforcements should be drawn from the National Resources Mobilization Act soldiers in Canada, the "zombies" as they were beginning to be called. (Zombies were horror movie creatures, soulless, mindless, walking dead—a term that some too clever "patriots" thought fitted the NRMA troops). Colonel Ralston told the stunned cabinet:

> I must say to Council, that while I am ready to explore the situation further, as I see it at the moment, I feel that there is no alternative but for me to recommend the extension of service of NRMA personnel to overseas.[6]

THE CRISIS IN CABINET

The fat was in the fire. After five years of war, the struggle at last was to be joined on the issue of conscription. With parliament not in session, the Tories could only watch from the sidelines while the Liberal cabinet fought over the question. How could Mackenzie King wiggle out of this issue, the issue that posed the greatest threat to national unity since 1917, the issue that seemed certain to split the Liberal party, and not least important, the issue that threatened to tumble the Prime Minister from the seat of power?

Immediately after Ralston had finished speaking, King indicated that he did not agree with his Minister of National Defence, and he polled his ministers. Three-quarters supported his position, but those opposed included some of the most important English-speaking ministers. The French-speaking cabinet members, of course, supported King against Ralston.

With Lapointe dead and Cardin gone since 1942, the most important of the Quebec ministers was undoubtedly Louis St. Laurent, the Minister of Justice. St. Laurent was a Quebec City lawyer who had been brought into the cabinet after Lapointe's death, although he had had no political experience. His integrity and fairmindedness, however, were such that he quickly became the senior Quebec representative, and in the conscription crisis that was to swirl around the cabinet chamber for the next six weeks, he was a key figure.

The conscriptionists were led by Ralston. The Minister of National Defence was a good man, an honest man, a solid man. He worked prodigious hours, labouring over every detail, and always vitally concerned for the welfare of the private soldier. He had favoured conscription from 1942 onward, but he had accepted Mackenzie King's pledge that when conscription was necessary it would be enforced. Now, Ralston said, conscription was necessary.

To the Prime Minister, this was still an arguable point. The war, after all, was almost over. Why jeopardize the unity of the country for the sake of sending only 15,000 reinforcements overseas? King wrote in his diary:

> . . . I shall be the one that will be pilloried on the one side by the Army and its friends . . . and on the other hand by the great majority of the people of Canada itself if, after the stand I have taken right along and with such success, I should permit a situation to develop that will help to destroy the unity of Canada for years to come and that to no avail so far as the winning of the war is concerned.

Clearly King had no intention of abandoning his no conscription policy without a fight. With a characteristic reference to the fact that God was on his side, he wrote:

> I believe that we shall get through without conscription and that the same power which has guided me in the past will continue to guide me through another very difficult period.[7]

Incredibly, as the crisis developed within the cabinet, it was discovered that in Canada there were no less than 120,000 volunteers for service anywhere and an additional 90,000 in England. And yet, said the Minister of National Defence and his staff officers, the necessary 15,000 reinforcements could not be drawn from this enormous pool of men but would have to come from some 60,000 NRMA soldiers in Canada. Could this have been correct? Could 15,000 infantrymen not be found among the more than 200,000 volunteers?

Incredibly they could not. According to General E. L. M. Burns in his book, *Manpower in the Canadian Army*, approximately 50,000 men were still in training and could not properly be pushed through their courses faster. Another 65,000 were in hospital, in headquarters staffs, or in various formations in the United Kingdom and were unavailable. A further 85,000 troops were either protecting key points, acting as instructors, or doing headquarters duties in Canada. The remainder for various reasons were considered "non-effectives" for battle purposes.[8] The military were satisfied that the necessary men could be found only from among the NRMA soldiers.

Thus, by the end of October the lines were hardened. Ralston was convinced that sending the NRMA soldiers overseas was essential. King was persuaded that it was not. The compromises had been explored and rejected, and the test of power was at hand. Mackenzie King was fighting for his political life now, and he had one further card to play.

General A. G. L. McNaughton was this last card. McNaughton had led the Canadian Army overseas until he was retired because of "ill health", after a series of squabbles with British officers. A "scientific" soldier, McNaughton had never believed that manpower was the answer to every military problem, and King knew of this. What a stroke it would be if McNaughton could be persuaded to enter the cabinet in place of Ralston. What a stroke, indeed, and the General agreed.

As a result, when the cabinet met on November 1, 1944, King calmly told Ralston that he was to be replaced by General McNaughton. Caught unawares by the Prime Minister's action, Ralston merely shook hands with his colleagues and left the cabinet room. His fellow conscriptionists were stunned into silence as King announced that McNaughton would put his enormous prestige into an all-out effort to persuade NRMA soldiers to volunteer for overseas duty. It appeared that King had carried the trick.

The game could yet be lost, however, and it all depended upon the NRMA troops. The 60,000 conscripts (of whom no

Lieutenant-General Andrew G. L. McNaughton, 1942.

"The most compelling Canadian personality of the war period was not a politician but a soldier—General A. G. L. McNaughton; and when, in an evil hour for himself, McNaughton went into politics, it was under conditions that made him ineffective."

C. P. Stacey, "Through the Second World War," in J. M. S. Careless and R. C. Brown, *The Canadians* (Toronto: Macmillan, 1967), pp. 278/79.

more than 35 percent were French-Canadian) had developed a certain perverse pride in their status. Scorned by press and politician as "zombies," they gloried in the name. "If the government wants us to go overseas," they jeered, "let them send us, but we will never volunteer to get the politicians off the hook." For more than three years the conscripts had been begged, pleaded with, shouted at to go overseas as volunteers. Hardened now, they refused. McNaughton met with no success. Between

November 1 and 18, only 549 men were persuaded to volunteer for overseas service. The game was as good as finished, although the General was not yet persuaded of this fact.

Other generals, however, were convinced that the recruiting drive was going to collapse. Some of them began saying so to the press. General George Pearkes, the commanding officer on the Pacific Coast, for example, called a press conference on November 20 and told his officers to tell the newspapers the truth. They did. The men would just not volunteer, they said. This act was close to rank insubordination, and there were signs that other generals were edging dangerously close to similar steps. Was discipline breaking down?

Perhaps. On November 22, the senior officers at Army Headquarters sent General McNaughton a memorandum saying that "the Voluntary system of recruiting through Army channels cannot meet the immediate problem." The General then telephoned the Prime Minister. King related the conversation in his diary:

> He said he had quite serious news. . . . That the Headquarters Staff here had advised him that the voluntary system would not get the men. . . . He expressed the opinion that it was like a blow in the stomach. He also said that he had the resignation of the Commander in Winnipeg. That if the Commanders, one after the other, began to resign, the whole military machine would run down, begin to disintegrate and there would be no controlling the situation.[9]

To King and McNaughton this situation must have seemed close to a military rebellion. Bruce Hutchison, the well-informed biographer of King, has said that King saw it as akin to a revolt of the generals.[10] Was it? Not really. General Maurice Pope, a close adviser to the Prime Minister and a staff officer at Army Headquarters, has stated that the senior officers acted merely as good public servants in advising their Minister that his policy could not be made to work.[11] But Professor R. MacGregor Dawson, King's official biographer, has charged that the senior officers timed their memorandum to take advantage of the session of parliament that was to begin the following

THE WEATHER
City and lower lakes region: Westerly winds; partly cloudy and cold. Low tonight, 30. High tomorrow, 35.

COMMONS TO HEAR ARMY NEEDS

COMMONS SUMMONED FOR CONFIDENCE VOTE

Premier King Will Ask House to Endorse Volunteer System—May Hear McNaughton in Secret Session on Reinforcement Situation

By H. R. ARMSTRONG

Ottawa, Nov. 14.—Premier King will submit the infantry reinforcement issue to the Canadian parliament on Nov. 22. The question raised in the published statement of Hon. J. L. Ralston, former minister of defence, is regard to sending drafthees overseas, is of such gravity that the prime minister feels the members of the House of Commons must be fuller informed at the earliest possible date, and requires their decision upon it.

Calling of the Commons for Nov. 22 instead of Jan. 31 now does not necessarily mean an early election. In government circles it is expected that the administration will receive a vote of confidence on the volunteer reinforcement issue...

HUMAN GUN TURRETS GO INTO ACTION IN THE SOUTH PACIFIC

GUN-TOTING SOLDIER BURIES HIS FACE AGAINST BLAST AS HIS MATE FIRES 30-CAL. MACHINE GUN

FIFTH FORT SEIZED NAZIS MAY FLEE METZ

U.S. Guns Cover Last Boltholes, While Patton's Moselle Troops Push Within 1½ Miles of Germany's Saar Frontier

Allied Supreme Headquarters, Nov. 14.—Another fortress group of Ver. four miles south of Metz, was captured by the U.S. 3rd Army today in a mounting sweep that carried American forces to within 3½ miles of the Moselle river city guarding the Saar valley.

The same success at Ver brought to five the number of Metz fortifications already overrun by the Americans. Earlier, the capture of Fort Orny had been announced at Moorville, the 3rd Army's left flank pushed forward to their Moselle bridgehead to within 1½ miles of the German frontier near the Luxembourg corner.

ROBOMBS BACK AGAIN LONDON IS DAMAGED

London, Nov. 14.—(AP)—After a lull of several days the Germans launched a robot flying bomb attack on southern England during last night. Some damage was done as the London area and in outlying districts.

The ministry of home security announced that 173 civilians were killed in air raids on the United Kingdom during October. Injured and released at hospital were listed at...

HOME AND SPORT EDITION

WINNIE'S NO SNOB USES GOERING BED

Paris, Nov. 14.—(BUP)—Prime Minister Churchill's secret visit to Paris must have brought him a bit of personal satisfaction over the liberation of France. While here Mr. Churchill slept in the same bed in the hotel once a great of Goering's when Herman stayed in the hotel during his stays in Paris during the German occupation.

It was disclosed unofficially that a bed in an adjoining room...

REINFORCE QUEBEC UNITS OFFER OF C.O.'S IN QUEBEC

ADMIT HITLER? DE VALERA WON'T SAY YES OR NO

London, Nov. 14.—(BUP)—The government of Eire has declined to give other neutral nations a revealing statement to prescribed Axis war criminals and has reserved the right to shelter such refugees in its own discretion, a government spokesman indicated in the House of Commons today.

Replying to a variety of questions from the House, Paul Emrys-Evans, undersecretary, said Eire had rejected the Allied demand that neutral states close their doors to war-guilty Axis leaders.

PANIC FOLLOWS ARREST OF NAZI BANKERS—SWEDE

Stockholm, Nov. 14.—The Gestapo has "arrested the managing directors of Germany's two greatest banks," causing a panic in German financial circles "greater than the panic following the bank crash in 1931," the newspaper Tidningen said today. The banker were Dr. Oswald Roesler, managing director of the Deutsche Bank and Karl Goetz, managing director of the Dresdner Bank.

SECOND COLUMN OF SOVIET TANKS NEARS BUDAPEST

Moscow, Nov. 14.—The Second Ukrainian army, completing the savage pincers around Budapest, today drove to within 28 miles of the Hungarian capital, driving German forces back...

VOKES EXPLAINS LEAVE PLAN TO CANADIANS ON ADRIATIC

With the Canadian Corps on the Adriatic, Nov. 14.—(CP)—Details of Canada's rotational plan of home leave for long-service men being explained to the troops by Maj.-Gen. Chris Vokes, commander, in a message to all ranks...

LADY NELSON DOCKS 24 HOURS AFTER AB

CANUCK BAGS 2 ME.'S AFTER BOMBING RA

12 CANADIAN FLIERS HELPED SINK TIRPITZ

London, Nov. 14.—(CP)—At least a dozen Canadian airmen participated in the R.A.F. Lancaster attack which sank the German battleship Tirpitz on Sunday. Included among them were F/O Walter Daniel, Rivers, Man., and (S/L) Johnny LeBoo, Toronto. Daniel bomb-aimer in the lead aircraft may have been the first to hit the Tirpitz...

CHURCHILL BACK IN LONDON

London, Nov. 14.—(BUP)—Prime Minister Winston Churchill returned late today from Paris, where he conferred with Gen. Charles de Gaulle and took part in the Armistice Day celebration.

LIQUID GLASS BY TON ESCAPES, STARTS FIRE

Special to The Star

Hamilton, Nov. 14.—Liquid glass spread over a wide area...

Bones of Death Camp Millions Used to Pave 'Black Death'...

Moscow, Nov. 14.—A "black road of death" surfaced with the bones of millions of victims of the German terror has been found near the notorious "death camp" at Maidanek in north-eastern Poland.

As this camp, several million people are stated to have been butchered and then cremated on huge wooden pyres.

Survivors said the Germans used a mixture of human ashes and bones...

Hear Large Numbers of Draftees Go Active After Andy's Speech

Ottawa, Nov. 14.—(CP)—Commanding officers from the recruiting military district expressed to Canada are in the capital for a conference, beginning today, with Hon. A. G. L. McNaughton, minister of defence.

The meeting has been described as a "normal procedure under such circumstances" and news Gen. McNaughton the necessity of making a trans-Canada tour. It also is believed to have some connection with the recruiting effort in the last three weeks.

It was initially learned he will begin his duties tomorrow in voluntary recruiting...

FAMED "DAM BUSTER" SQUADRON OF THE R.A.F. SINKS THE TIRPITZ WITH SIX-TON EARTHSHAKER

TWO CANADIAN men here of the R.A.F. "Dam Buster" Squadron stand by a 12,000 pound bomb such as sank the Tirpitz. Their Lancasters can be seen on the airfield.

PRIDE OF Germany's fleet and practically immobile in Nazi-held harbors ever since her commissioned, this is the Tirpitz, whose 41,000 tons now lie at bottom of Tromso Fjord, Nor.

day.[12] Again General Pope rejects this charge, saying that Dawson credits the officers with a more highly developed political sense than they in fact possessed.[13]

Whatever the truth, there can be no doubt of Mackenzie King's reaction:

> It is apparent to me that to whatever bad management this may have been due, we are faced with a real situation which has to be met and now there is no longer thought as to the nature of the military advice tendered, particularly by General McNaughton.

In other words, King was saying, McNaughton now had to recommend that conscription be imposed. If this was the case, King noted, "it will be my clear duty to agree to the passing of the Order-in-Council," sending NRMA soldiers overseas. To not do so could lead to civil war.[14]

The significance then of the staff officer's memorandum is very clear. Revolt or not, King used the memorandum to justify for himself the amazing about-turn he was making. Whereas he had been adamantly opposed to conscription up to November 22, now he was in favour of it. He would send 16,000 NRMA soldiers overseas, but no more at this time. The most likely explanation for this switch, however, is not the "revolt of the generals" but sheer political reality. King knew that he had run out of expedients and delaying tactics. To maintain his opposition to conscription would be to defeat his government; this far he would not go.

King's assessment was correct. At the very time he was changing his mind, the conscriptionist ministers were meeting privately. Under the leadership of T. A. Crerar, the Minister of Mines, they were considering whether or not they should jointly submit their resignations to the Prime Minister. With his usual acute feel for the situation, King was probably aware of this. Almost certainly he knew that if four or five ministers were to resign his fate was sealed. The only way was to switch.

◄ The front page of the *Toronto Daily Star* for 14 November 1944.

Now King's task was to keep the anti-conscriptionists in the cabinet. If he could not do this, resignation and defeat were once again the only alternative. The key was St. Laurent. King told him of the generals' "revolt," almost certainly exaggerating the danger. St. Laurent was convinced that the war could be won without Canada's imposing conscription, his biographer, Dale Thomson, has said, but he was aware that if he failed to make the correct response the government would fall. The choice was to introduce a measure of moderate conscription or to see King replaced by someone who could only be worse— at least insofar as conscription was concerned. Under the circumstances, St. Laurent said that he would support the Prime Minister.[15]

"Chubby" Power, the Minister of National Defence for Air, was not so accommodating. Unlike St. Laurent who had not been in the cabinet then, Power had campaigned against Duplessis in 1939 on the specific promise that he would never support conscription. His pledges had been repeated in the 1940 election and again during the campaign for the plebiscite in 1942. To his credit, Power decided that he had no option, and he resigned.

Power was as aware as any man in Canada of the emotional nature of the conscription question. His son had been captured at Hong Kong by the Japanese, and he knew what fear was from his experiences in the Great War. Power knew that English-speaking Canadians were afraid for their sons overseas; he knew that because of this fear they would despise French Canadians who refused to enlist. But he also knew Quebec, and he understood the requirements of national unity. In a memorandum that he prepared after his resignation, Power stated the issue as he saw it:

> Conscription was a long way from being necessary at this stage. It was certainly convenient to send the Zombies, but convenience should give way before National interest. . . . I envisaged the prospect of one-third of our population unco-operative, with a deep sense of injury, and the prey to the worst elements among them, and worst of all hating all other Canadians.

And Power concluded with a quote from the Prime Minister:

> Conscription in the mind of the French Canadian, as such,
> is not so bad. It is because it is considered to be a symbol
> of British domination that it is anathema. To them it
> means being forced to fight for the 'maudit Anglais'. [16]

The loss of "Chubby" Power was important, but with St. Laurent staying at his side, King could weather the storm. Nonetheless, when he rose to address the House of Commons on November 27, King turned his back on the opposition benches and spoke directly to his own French-Canadian M.P.'s:

> If there is anything to which I have devoted my political
> life, it is to try to promote unity, harmony and amity be-
> tween the diverse elements of this country. My friends can
> desert me, they can remove their confidence from me, they
> can withdraw the trust they have placed in my hands, but
> never shall I deviate from that line of policy. Whatever
> may be the consequences, whether loss of prestige, loss of
> popularity, or loss of power, I feel that I am in the right,
> and I know that a time will come when every man will
> render me full justice on that score.[17]

This was a brilliant and moving speech, almost certainly one of the high points of King's oratorical career, and it was effective. Of fifty-seven French-Canadian members of parliament voting on the government's policy, twenty-three supported King, a strikingly high number in view of the opposition to conscription in Quebec.

Though violent for a time, the Canadien response was not as sharp as it had been in 1917. There was some rioting in Quebec City and in Montreal; Louis St. Laurent's home on Grand Allée in the Quebec capital was put under police guard; and the Quebec legislature passed a resolution censuring the federal government and regretting that King had violated his *engagements les plus sacrés*. But the feared bloodshed in the streets never occurred. The French Canadian took this new humiliation at the hands of the English sullenly but quietly.

To the Conservatives in parliament and out, King's policy was typically half-hearted. Forced out of his position of complete opposition to conscription by sheer necessity (as they saw it) he had taken a compromise position by sending only 16,000 conscripts overseas. This was just not good enough, and the Conservative press was violent in its denunciations of King's temporizing. Arthur Meighen was foaming with rage:

> Of all the pitiful performances known in the history of a great country, the senseless convolutions of the last three weeks take all prizes. . . . It is dishonest and foul trickery of the meanest kind.[18]

In fact, the Conservative rage directed at King did much to mollify Quebec. After all, Quebeckers reasoned, if the Tories were unhappy King must have done something right. The Conservatives could have killed the Liberals in Quebec, *Maclean's Magazine* pointed out. When King sent over the conscripts, the opposition should have congratulated the government on enforcing conscription at last. Instead, the magazine said, by attacking the King government policy, the Conservatives made it clear that the voluntary system was still in effect. They had shown Quebec that there was, in fact, a clear difference between total conscription and the limited step taken by King.[19]

In fact, the anger against King was fast dying. When passion cooled, French Canadians could see that after all King had done all he could to put off conscription as long as possible. As Michel Brunet, the distinguished French-Canadian historian, said long after the war:

> No one could deny that Mackenzie King and his colleagues had paid attention to French Canadian opinion. They had tried to prevent a violent conflict between the races. Most French Canadians were aware of this.[20]

*   *   *

As events turned out, the manpower shortage overseas eased off considerably. The first drafts of NRMA soldiers left for Europe in late December, 1944, and the soldiers reached the front lines in February, 1945. But because the Canadian forces were not heavily engaged over the New Year period, casualties were not excessive. As a result, only 2,463 conscripts served at the front, where they did as well as any other soldiers. It was a tame ending to the controversy and strife of five years.

Chapter V

The End of an Issue

Mackenzie King had brought the nation through one of its most difficult periods—not quite unscarred, but in better shape than many observers might have expected. He had done so, his critics in the Conservative party charged, only by deliberately and flagrantly catering to the will of the Province of Quebec. And he had done so, they added, at the risk of damaging the fighting capabilities of the Canadian Army in Europe. The crisis of 1944 was over, but the issue lingered on.

POLITICS AFTER THE CRISIS

The first victim of the anger of the Conservative party—and it must be added of a widespread resentment among English Canadians—was General McNaughton. Although the General had been named Minister of National Defence in November, he was not a Member of Parliament and could not address the House of Commons unless special dispensations were granted. Obviously, McNaughton had to get into parliament, and he ran in the first available by-election, which took place in the Ontario constituency of Grey North in the first week of February, 1945.

The Tories threw the book at the Minister. Their resentment was all the sharper at McNaughton because he had been carrying on conversations with key figures in their party about the possibility of his becoming Conservative leader at the very time he became Defence Minister. By "turning traitor," he forfeited any claims to Conservative consideration, and he was assailed mercilessly. The entire conscription crisis was laid at his door, and he was assailed along with Prime Minister King for allowing Quebec to escape scot-free.

The most damaging charge that was hurled at McNaughton,

however, came in a speech by John Bracken, the Conservative leader. Speaking at Meaford, Bracken demanded that the General *"tell you why some of those* [NRMA] *men arrived in Britain without their rifles which they are expected to have.* Let him tell you about how they threw their rifles—their ammunition overboard. Let him tell you the truth which is a condemnation of the complacency, the lack of leadership, the inept mishandling of the entire manpower problem in this nation."[1]

Bracken's damning, but totally unverified, statement was picked up by the international press and received wide coverage in the United States. Senator Burton Wheeler of Montana raised it in the United States Senate in question with a sentence of death that had been passed on an American G.I. for refusing to drill. "If that were done," Wheeler trumpeted, "between 16,000 and 18,000 Canadians would have to be hanged because of the fact that they refused to drill. Some of them apparently threw their arms overboard."[2] In fact, one private soldier had tossed his rifle and kitbags over the side as he boarded ship at Halifax, and according to his court martial there were signs of mental instability in his background. General McNaughton's rebuttal of the Bracken charges, however, never caught up with the accusation.

McNaughton made some errors of his own, too. He came into the riding to do his electioneering in a private railway car. This was not for the sake of his personal comfort, but because the car had special radio equipment that allowed him to keep in touch with the Department of National Defence in Ottawa. But to the rural voters of Grey North, this just didn't look right. In addition, the General's wife was a Roman Catholic, and this became the subject of a whisper campaign in the solidly Protestant constituency. Nothing went right for General McNaughton, and he was defeated by 7,333 votes for the Tory candidate, Garfield Case, to 6,097.

The Conservative party was jubilant at the victory. The sole issue had been reinforcements, and the issue obviously was a winner. If General McNaughton with his position as a minister of the Crown, his reputation as a soldier, and the full support of the Liberal party could be defeated, no Liberal was safe anywhere in Canada. Or so thought the Tories.

THE RETREAT FROM NORTH GREY

"When the moment arrives that my staff advises me that I am wanted in Ottawa for the business of war, I will pack up my bags and go, even though it may mean that I must miss the biggest meeting of my campaign."

A cartoon from *The Telegram*, Toronto, Monday, 29 January 1945.

The Conservatives would have a chance to test their popularity soon enough. Gambling that the war in Europe would be over by then, Prime Minister King announced June 11, 1945, as the date for the general election. It was a typically shrewd, Mackenzie King gamble—as it turned out, V-E Day came on May 8. As far as the Liberals were concerned, victory in Europe ended the reinforcement question as a burning political question. Now they could campaign on postwar issues like social security, stressing their plans for reconstruction and waving the baby bonus cheques that were beginning to go out to mothers across the country.

The Conservatives found themselves in a somewhat uncomfortable position when it came time to choose their election issues. They had endorsed social security at Port Hope in September, 1942, and at their Winnipeg convention in December of the same year. But because King was in office, he had received credit for implementing such social security measures as had been passed into legislation. Now if the Conservatives continued to play up this issue, they believed, they would seem to be saying "me, too." This, as every politician knows, is a dangerous position in which to be.

The other Tory issue, of course, was conscription. But with the war in Europe over, how could the issue be used? The war in the Pacific was still going on, however, and although Canada had not taken much part in this theatre, the government was preparing a force of some 15,000 men for service there. In his first major speech of the campaign, therefore, Bracken promised to carry out Canada's "fair share of responsibility" in the Pacific and to use physically fit conscript soldiers to carry out Canadian commitments.[3] Once again, with fatal timing, the Conservative party had nailed conscription to the masthead.

This move was a mistake of the first order. Rightly or wrongly, there was absolutely no enthusiasm in Canada for a major effort in the Pacific. The war there was regarded as an American affair, and while few objected to sending some Canadian troops to oppose Japan, the popular opinion was that the fewer sent the better. The result was that the Conservatives appeared to be a hyper-imperialistic party, looking for a fight even when no fight was necessary.

Equally significant, the party's announcement of support for conscription for the Pacific indicated that Conservatives had written off Quebec in this election. Indeed, there was very little left to write off. Maurice Duplessis had been returned to power at the head of a Union Nationale government in 1944, and he was believed to be sympathetic to the federal Conservatives.

Sympathetic, yes, but not crazy. Once the Conservatives began riding the conscription horse, Duplessis' organizers very quickly disappeared from the Conservative ranks. It could come as no surprise, therefore, when Duplessis announced that the Union Nationale supported no federal party, and when former Conservatives vehemently denounced Bracken as an imperialist.

As a result there were few Quebec Conservatives left to object when Bracken and other leading party figures began to use the race issue as a weapon. Bracken told a cheering audience in Oshawa, Ontario:

> They have drained your firesides of your sons and they have deceived Quebec in this war. The government has now announced that it will expect the war in the Pacific to be fought by those who volunteer. The government's policy in this respect is but another bid for Quebec's support. They are asking your sons to die in double the numbers of others and they are asking Quebec to continue to be misrepresented before the world. The patriotic among Canada's sons will again be asked to die for Canada, while others will stay at home to populate the land their brother's saved.[4]

This reference to the "revenge of the cradle" was pretty strong stuff, and so was the charge in an *Ottawa Journal* editorial of June 5:

> Mr. King had been campaigning in Quebec, and winning support in Quebec, and continuing himself in office because of Quebec, through appeals to Quebec's prejudices. It is one of the ugly, tragic things of Canadian politics.

There were some elements of truth in the Conservative attacks, but their force was weakened by the support the party gave to anti-conscriptionist Independents in thirty-three Quebec ridings. These nationalist candidates, a Quebec organizer for the party said, differ with official policy only on "points which are not essential."[5] Conscription, evidently, was not essential.

The Conservative-*nationaliste* alliance gave Mackenzie King

INDEX
Amusements—11   Radio—18
Births, Deaths—12   Legal—II-25
Comics—18   Want Ads—11-25
Markets—12   Women—21-22

TORONTO DAILY STAR

53RD YEAR

TORONTO, TUESDAY, JUNE 12, 1945—32 PAGES

THE WEATHER
Toronto and vicinity, Wednesday:
Fair and moderately warm. Low
tonight 56, high tomorrow, 74.

3c PER COPY, 18c PER WEEK

VICTORY FOR UNITY, KING SAYS

**Last Word on 64 Seats
Coming From Soldiers**

HOME AND SPORT EDITION

750,000 SOLDIER VOTES MAY DECIDE 64 SEATS

Overseas Ballots Could Change Results for Prime
Minister King, Gardiner, Mackenzie and Sir
Henry Drayton—Majorities Now Small

By THE CANADIAN PRESS

Key to the Canadian general election is the vote of an estimated 750,000 service personnel, to be announced June 20. A compilation by the Canadian Press shows the final decision in 64 seats may rest on the service vote.

The seats comprise 38 in which the election of Liberals was indicated by the civilian vote, 18 Progressive Conservative, eight C.C.F. and eight others.

FOR WHAT HE DID, WHAT HE WILL DO CANADA AGAIN SAYS 'YES' TO KING

Prime Minister's Liberal Government Given Representation From Every Province From Atlantic
to Pacific—Drew-Bracken Attacks Fail

By H. R. ARMSTRONG

Ottawa, June 12—Canadians yesterday returned Premier Mackenzie King and his Liberal government to direct their affairs until Japan is beaten and our postwar problems are solved.

In an unprecedented electoral triumph, the King government survived the fierce fourfold split upon it to emerge a truly national administration, armed with a mandate to maintain its domestic and international programme.

Victory—only a scant vague in the Ontario elections, the MacCallugh-Drew-Bracken machinery forces suffered a severe setback at the hands of the Canadian voters.

Premier King hailed the verdict as a success for national unity. "What perhaps has brought to the present administration in such measure the support which has come to it today from all parts of Canada," he said, "is the extent to which national unity has been maintained throughout the years of war. You have taken the opportunity to show the world that unity still appeals to races, creed, and economic interest and the pinning of prejudices and prejudices may be the rock in trade of a certain order of politicians; every true Canadian regards all who make such appeals as enemies of their own unity and indeed enemies of mankind."

FROM COAST TO COAST

In every province of the Dominion the verdict of the electors returned Liberals to the next parliament. From Prince Edward Island to British Columbia without exception the King government was accorded the full of Commons representation. Even in Ontario where the Drew forces won a sweeping ministry victory last Monday, the King administration elected at least 33 representatives. The Liberals only carried all but two of the King cabinet ministers back into office. The Canadian prime minister himself carried the riding of Prince Albert in a close contest. Significant also the attitude of the Canadian people was the victory of Hon. Humphry Mitchell minister of labor, in Welland and the success of Hon. C. DeCourcy, Reconstruction minister, in Port Arthur. These were two of the few seats which national Liberal headquarters recognized as focal points of the struggle.

The return of the King cabinet ministers bores an its triumphant. Montreal, indicated the national character of the Liberal achievement.

OUTSTANDING STATESMAN

The result of yesterday's voting stamps Premier King as the outstanding Canadian statesman. By the time he has finished his current mandate as prime minister he will have headed the nation for a longer time than Sir John A. Macdonald, his closest rival in terms of years.

Canadians who faced the Dominion provincial election was a signal for seizure to reactionary policies throughout Canada were heartened by the results of yesterday's voting. Premier King made it plain throughout his campaign tag, he was compelled to inaugurate social and war postwar legislation. This was no direct retreat to the programme of his Drew government which based its appeal on opposition to forward looking, policy.

It was equally a setback to those groups in the province of Quebec which sought to capitalize on separatist, anti-British sentiment for partisan purposes.

TRIUMPH IN QUEBEC

Perhaps the greatest 'achievement of the prime minister in yesterday's voting was that the repudiation of French-speaking cabinet ministers who stood unyieldingly with him in the imposition of overseas conscription for military service. Never before in Canadian history have French-Canadian cabinet ministers given their support to compulsory service outside Canada.

Despite the nationalists' appeal to the race of the King government presents, Hon. Louis St. Laurent, Hon Ernest Bertrand, Hon. Alphonse Fournier, and other Quebec cabinet ministers were returned by their constituents. Wilfred English-speaking Quebec cabinet ministers, Hon. Brooke Claxton and Hon. D. C. Abbott were re-elected in ridings to which the Brackenites made especially strong appeals.

If there is one thing more than another that stands out in yesterday's balloting, it is that Premier King and his government carried with them into the next five years the support of people of wildly-varying views on the issues of war as well as the problems of peace. John Bracken, Progressive Conservative leader, resorted to the time-worn tactics of appealing to sectional prejudices and interests. But this trends he found himself unable to make a single national note-broadcast during the campaign.

PREACHED NATIONAL UNITY

Premier King, on the other hand, spoke his philosophy of national unity, international co-operation and an all-out war effort to every part of Canada. That he could carry the country at this stage of affairs by such an appeal is the happiest augury for the future of Canada as a nation that has yet been demonstrated in a national election.

While John Bracken was labelling Premier King and his policy as "cowardly and degraded," and criticising his appeal to suit the sectional before whom he appeared. Mr. King adhered to his national program whenever he moved.

That was a straightforward account of what Canada had accomplished in the war and what his government promised and had accomplished for social and economic security for every element in Canada. This consistency in all the same time the strength and weakness of his appeal to the electors and many of his foremost supporters feel that he best sacrificed policies to statesmanship.

Considering the long time Premier King has been in office this was a signature fate on the part of those who knew that democratic machine like to courage governments with reasonable frequency. The supreme shows that the Canadian public can be trusted to endorse without limit those who honestly attempt to improve their domestic and international standard.

IMPETUS TO NEW DEAL

The Canadian new deal, given additional impetus during the war years, is safe for further expansion during the coming years of peace. The emergence fiscal policies of the government, backed by the temporary but equally important aggressive war program, has received the backing of voters all across Canada.

The attempts of Progressive Conservatives to cash in on social, social and economic appeal in the Dominion under the guise of assuring Premier King of being an enemy of national unity, has apathy failed. The campaign of hate, vituperation which the opposition thought has won so strikingly in Ontario, fell flat when Mr. King's experiment attempted to apply it on a national scale.

Upon yesterday's results no one can say that the King administration rests upon the foundation stock of Quebec or any other

(Continued on Page 2, Col. 4)

PARTY STANDINGS YESTERDAY, TODAY

Comparative standings of parties:
Dissolution   Today

Liberal	155	119
Ind.-Lib.	5	4
C.C.F.	8	26
Soc. Cred.	10	12
Prog.-Cons.	39	65
Lab.-Prog.		1
Lib.-Prog.		2
Ind.	12	10
Vacant	12	
In doubt		8
	245	245

AS GALLUP POLL SAID, LIBERALS GOT 39 PER CENT.

Ottawa, June 12 — Incomplete civilian-vote compilations today indicated that Liberal candidates polled 39 per cent, exactly as the Gallup Poll predicted it would. According to the 1944 division, the Liberals polled 41 per cent, of the vote and 44 per cent in 1935.

According to the Canadian Press compilation, Progressive Conservatives polled 28 per cent, compared to 31 per cent, in 1940 as National Government candidates. The Conservatives percentage in 1935 was 30.

The C.C.F. party percentage took it compared with eight per cent, in 1940 and nine per cent in 1935. The percentage vote figures to understand the C.C.F.'s success in popular polls reporting, showed that the election vote gains were offset by a reaction of 4,620,000 cast compared to the 1940 record of 4,610,000 if our total in the highest figure in history.

Gallup Sampling Accurate

(By Canadian Institute of Public Opinion)

Official election returns about 90 per cent complete, offer once again striking evidence not only of the accuracy of modern opinion sampling method as employed by the Gallup Poll, but also of their objectivity.

Latest returns on the national election compare with the Gallup Poll forecast of last Saturday as follows:

	Gallup Margin of error	Actual Results Forecast
Liberals		41% 37%
Prog.-Cons.		29 28
C.C.F.		15 15
Others		18 20

Average margin of error : 2.7
The limitation, as it had forecast, drew 8 per cent, in the West Prog.-Conser. Canadian. It was not needed to announce Miss Populistic from "others" as early returns.

Comparison of minimum to Ontario and Quebec with Gallup Poll forecasts from earlier returns became available:

NO PERSON IN BERLIN ADMITS BEING NAZI

By HENRY SHAPIRO

Berlin, June 12—BUP—Nazis are as rare in Berlin as they are in Mascow—to hear the people of Berlin tell it.

After questioning Germans at random on the streets here, one would think that not one of Berlin's 3,500,000 inhabitants ever joined, supported, or sympathized with the Nazi movement.

"Hitler Kaput" has replaced "Heil Hitler" as the greeting of the day. In 1939 I saw all Berlin hit the streets shouting, cheering and swearing loyalty to the Weimar republic. In successive years after 1945, I saw the same Berliners goose-stepping as Unter Den Linden and hysterically hailing Hitler.

Now if the Allies had their way, hated people here could not recall the same Berliners confidentially if had their Odhausen.

The German events report that not one wall but they do not before the meat of guilt.

Even the communist now wears his Adolf Wanfrost appreciably a shrewder anti-Nazi—or not at all applicable for German moment.

The only German I met who openly admitted Germany's war guilt was Otto Grisham, a former Communist member of the Weimar Reichstag and a German of 17 years in concentration camps.

LONDON LAUGHS LAST AS 'HAW-HAW' ON WAY

London, June 12—William Joyce was broadcast as "Lord Haw-Haw" over the Hamburg radio during the war, will be brought to London today, and broadcast in, the Evening Standard said. It said he as a military prisoner could be at any time. Then he will be handed over to Scotland Yard.

WILLIAM LYON MACKENZIE KING

—Photo by Karsh

WOMEN CAN RULE, SAYS THE ONE WOMAN ELECTED

Qu'Appelle, Sask., June 12—In defeating Defence Minister Gen. A. G. L. McNaughton, Mrs. Gladys Strum, farmer's wife, is convinced that her success at the polls is due in part to her firm belief that women are people.

"No use time if I campaign for women's rights," she said today. "I campaigned for people's rights. I have always believed that women were people, and I campaigned for people's rights—the rights of men, women, and children."

In her constituency a great many people explains that they would have their own representative, one would represent their viewpoint, her division.

Mrs. Corn Casselman, Liberal member for Edmonton East and delegate to the San Francisco security conference, was defeated by Patrick Ashen, Social Credit candidate. Another woman member of parliament, Miss Dorise Nielsen, a Labor-Progressive candidate, was defeated in North Battleford.

A farmer's wife and ex-school teacher, with a 11-year-old daughter, Mrs. Strum says she has no political ambitions. She ran for parliament because she was confident.

"I am president of the C.C.F. in Saskatchewan. I was chairman of the continuing meeting. I was one member of this body's radio committee. If Mrs. expects to achieve democratic then I must accept responsibilities. Mr. Husband is very pleased with my success. He always has been interested in progressive movement and very active in the party. He was responsible for my interest in politics."

"The Anne-coup began an official in making statement of the last major Japanese stronghold in the Pacific might fall within two or three weeks yet would generally be deferred."

BORNEO AUSSIES GAIN IN ASSAULT ON BIG OIL FIELD

Manila, June 12—Australian troops, rapidly expanding their seaside compulsions bridge head on northwest Borneo today pushed into the great Scrum Bay field section, an area that they had seen as the great Tarakan oil centre today. Gen. MacArthur reported today.

In fighting described as involving heavy ground and air action, troops already moved in the north Brunei Bay area. The MacArthur forces swept through the rich petroleum area nearby. Fully four enemy bombers were encountered at the rich landing field.

The big Serita oil field—about the rich petroleum are the Borneo—lies seven miles inland of the assault, and mile from the first Japanese force trapped in a Big rail interior. Justly the rich oil field centre were in tapping. Parity for the oil fields outside of Brunei town.

The Australians drove down the Brunei-on-Borneo road against Unita miles line of Borneo lines outside of at Mir at of the big landing near an capital at the rapid advance of their whole.

A new invasion front was heralded by the Australians at their landings. They pressed forward where resistance was wooden comic leeward the strenuous made it impossible for the battle to get close robust. Within three hits point of the war the vision pushed south the rich and the oil gum as measured and weaving.

Another U.S. landing on the southern beaches of Okinawa mile south completed occupation of island, U.S. troops, after thrust in the Japanese force began to a field plateau, over reported today in Washington. This government the force reported down 130 to 836 but climb between down 220 to 645 to chase a division.

U.S. forces pressed in within Moving stronghold of the last major Japanese stronghold in the Pacific might fall within two or three weeks yet would be deferred.

THE WEATHER

TUESDAY-WEDNESDAY

Moderate winds; fair to Moderate variable winds. Fair and moderately warm today and front of Wednesday; little rain temperature change in eastern districts.

Official weather data:
Highest temperature, at 3.00 p.m. 73
Lowest temperature, p.m., 56.
Barometer, 30.15 at 8 a.m.
8 a.m. today, rising.
Lowest temperature at 7:50 a.m. 53.
Lowest this morning at 4 a.m. 53.
Sun rises tomorrow at 5:12 a.m.
Sun sets tonight at 8:51 p.m.

Toronto Calendar
Sun rises tomorrow at 5:12, D.S.T.
Sun sets tonight at 8:51, D.S.T.

'Duck or You'll Get Shot' MacArthur Remains Standing

Melbourne, Australia, June 12—at all but the free grenade dropped when Australian reinforcements will be 20 yards off. Gen. Douglas MacArthur was ashore on Japanese-near-sniper-swept, with a notice front a mile behind him as it fell. The rest within three quarters of a mile of the actual fighting in a number of Japanese Bombers within a mile behind him.

MacArthur and Macleod troops and Australian commanders near him. Two of them were killed by the sniper, staff one and Japanese troops; and equal to flushing out Japanese positions in their respective lines.

BENNETT VISITS MONTREAL

Montreal, June 12—(CP)—Viscount Bennett, former Conservative prime minister of Canada, arrived here today from his country estate at Juniper, England, via Saint John, N.B., and planned to visit Ottawa before sailing to his home in Mickleham, Surrey, England. He left Monday.

CHINA'S MATA HARI EXECUTED AS SPY

Chungking, June 11—(BUP)—The Chinese government has shared the most dramatic spy case of the Far East war. The Democratic Chinese Mata Hari—Miss Chen Den Ero—has been executed as a traitress.

Miss Chen had only all military information for the Japanese, but tried on many occasions to induce Chinese officers to desert to the enemy forces.

Candidates listed as "others" in Quebec are three Independents, two Independent Liberals, one Independent Conservative and one Bloc Populaire.

Most prominent of the doubtful candidates is Prime Minister King whose majority in Prince Albert was 280. The agriculture minister, Hon. James G. Gardiner, with a majority of 225 in Melville and Hon. Ian Mackenzie, minister of veterans' affairs with a 1,687 majority over a Chinese Vancouver North winner. B. and M. Jones Churchill too.

One with a larger known of a 1,627 voters doubtful is Thomas Reid, Liberal. Returned in Revelstoke with 2,211 majority.

VOTE PUTS CANADA BACK ON TWO-PARTY SYSTEM

By H. B. ARMSTRONG

Ottawa, June 12—One of the distinct trends of the federal voting yesterday was the curtailment of expansion of political power other than the two traditional parties.

In this respect the minister election result reflects the feeling in the Ontario general election held last week. The Quebec provincial voting of last year.

The Bloc Populaire in Quebec, whose ubiquitous was heralded in the provincial election, all but was wiped out as a political force in the general voting to come over the ballot on the federal politics parties here and in Quebec. Yesterday the C.C.F extended its meagre representation in Quebec of a low, and the political party which now has all the general ground in, Canada's west. The Bloc as a whole in, the west only polling 2,000 vote.

The Social Credit party, entrenched in Alberta, while at home.

THE KING GIVES IKE EXCLUSIVE ORDER

London, June 12—The King today invested Gen. Dwight D. Eisenhower with the Order of Merit. The supreme Allied commander is the first U.S. soldier ever to receive the exclusive honor of the Not members of the order either 24 civil and military, limited to 24.

The King gave 24 Australian earnings and Guardsmen at an investiture, June 12.

... nationally was in the King government, ... Independent voters in eight of Canada's nine provinces and to a considerable extent in Ontario elected to the Liberal party as the party best suited to serve their and their interests during this postwar and reconstruction period.

There is no gainsaying that the progress of the C.C.F. has been comparatively slight to that which was expected by many of its most ardent supporters. The C.C.F. remains the balance of power in the dominion. This is a continuing feature in Canada. To meet and ask in total their today's group, will not only depends as four developments.

RETURNED MEN WILL FIGHT $500,000 ILLEGAL FUR TRAFFIC

Illegal beaver and fur trapping in Ontario has now created a racket amounting to $250,000 to $500,000 yearly, Hon. George Dunbar, minister of game and fisheries, said today. Police valued at approximately $33,000, found by provincial police on an abandoned mail in the far-flung puttis-Oil Lake region, the largest seizure in five years, have reached the northern buildings. The government is raising the moment fire to deal that from $50 to $50 for illegal beaver skins raise to $30 per head of illegally-trapped fur. The government will bring in a whole lot of those as large as the beaver.

Recently the department of game and fisheries have dealt with illegal-pelter furs and a larger quantity will be put on the market for our sale of it.

The police to illegal furs is comparable to be speaking in silver and blue gone in the south. A beaver pelt brings about $65 on the legitimate market and only $30 to $40 to a racketeer handler.

NOT THE MAN ASSAULTED

George Essay at Crawford St. stated today he was not assaulted — nor "ruffian" on Bayview Ave., Riverdale. The men reported Monday. Some else of the same name were not men.

SELL PATROL ON 'HONOR'

Ottawa, June 12—(CP)—Garage and gasoline-oil operators of the Ottawa district at a meeting last night voted to continue the 3 am. to 9 p.m. hours of sale for gasoline under the honor system, not to open for customer's over on Sunday. The meeting also decided that no party need a gas-station and the national government control in fewer cases than now being limited when rationing of gasoline and oil, were then lifted recently.

$5 U-BOATS STILL UNACCOUNTED FO[R]

Washington, June 12—A navy surgeon operational disclosed today that five German submarines are still unaccounted for in Atlantic waters, but it seems certain the five Nazi submersibles at the bottom of the ocean. Two of the unaccounted-for German craft may have escaped to Argentina but they be unlikely to offer themselves in the event of the Germans fled.

PONY DRAGS BOY, 12, ON TRACK DEATH-RI[DE]

Special to the Star

Midland, June 12—Dragged a mile which he saved about his cart, an Ontario boy, Bob Rowe,ranger on his farm here, was dragged to his death in the country at noon hour near Town Centre. The boy, son of Mr. and Mrs. George Rowe, the pony by halter leading and some way.

GIRL'S PURSE SNATCHED

Special to the Star

A purse containing $7, taken from her by Jessie MacVannel has been recovered police stated today reported the pony dragged the young girl pulled around a back of the rear near Shaw St. station, and a boy was seized as it passed.

the opportunity for which he had been looking. He told a cheering Montreal crowd:

> I saw the defeat of Sir Wilfrid Laurier in 1911, a defeat caused by the alliance of the nationalists of this province with the Tories of the other provinces.[6]

Liberal advertisements in the Quebec French-language press blared:

> Bracken and the Conservative party are the party of high tariffs and low salaries. They are the natural enemy of Quebec, and they betrayed us in 1911 and 1917. They are running their campaign on the backs of French Canadians.[7]

If Conservative prospects in Quebec were dead and buried, there were grounds for optimism in Ontario. There Premier George Drew had won a sweeping election victory on June 4, just one week before the federal election date. Drew was an adamant conscriptionist, and his victory was interpreted as a clear sign that Ontario would go Conservative federally.

So it did. In Ontario the Conservatives elected forty-eight MPs out of the province's eighty-two representatives. In Quebec, however, only two Tories were returned. Nationally, the totals were 127 for the Liberals, 68 for the Conservatives and 22 for the CCF. Mackenzie King had won again. The Conservative party had been defeated once more by conscription.

THE CRISIS IN RETROSPECT

There can be no doubt of the significance of the issue of conscription. Twice in the twentieth century it came close to destroying national unity. Twice it tore apart political parties. Twice it divided French Canadian from English Canadian. But equally there can be no doubt that the conscription crises of the Second World War were not as damaging as that of 1917.

◀ The front page of the *Toronto Daily Star* for 12 June 1945.

Why? It is too simplistic to say that the difference was Mackenzie King, but there is much truth in this. King was a political animal who lived and breathed politics. He was not above
political trickery—as when he sprang a snap election on Manion
in January, 1940. He was not above ruthlessness—as when he
wielded the axe on Colonel Ralston on November 1, 1944.
Clearly, King could be an unpleasant man. But he had a dream.
He saw that unity between English and French Canada was
essential, and he saw that conscription, involving as it did
the deepest emotions of both nations, was one of the few issues
that could sever relations between Quebec and the rest of the
country.

This was the greatest motivation for his wartime policy: prevent conscription to preserve unity. As a policy it was dangerous
at times for King. If Meighen had been a more skilful politician, he might have been able to create a situation in which
King would have had to step down in 1942. If Ralston had cared
to campaign against King after the November, 1944 crisis, he
probably could have brought down the Prime Minister. But
Meighen was incapable of mounting a sustained attack and
Ralston would not. King was saved in some respects by his opponents' weaknesses.

King's policy was by no means a glamorous one. It looked,
frankly, silly for a country to have two armies—one for fighting
and one for home defence. It was wasteful in terms of equipment, money and training time. It took men out of industry and
agriculture where they could be usefully employed and stuck
them in NRMA battalions where they did nothing. But it was
necessary, necessary for French Canada, necessary for Canada.

And when King finally was forced out of his carefully constructed position by the 1944 conscription crisis, it was clear
to Quebec that he had done all he could. He had done as much
as any man could do. That is why the Liberals captured fifty-six
of the sixty-five Quebec seats in the 1945 general election. King
had remembered 1917 when the country was divided and when
Quebec had gone virtually without representation in the cabinet. He had remembered, and even more, he had learned.

The same could not be said for the opposition party. The
Conservatives had learned nothing from the experience of the

Great War. Conscription had been rammed down Quebec's throat then, and they were convinced that the medicine should be repeated in the Second World War. As the only major figure in the party whose career spanned the two wars, Arthur Meighen had to assume the major responsibility for this Conservative policy. Meighen had drafted the conscription legislation of 1917 and had led the fight for its passage in that year. He had been right then, he firmly believed, and to prove it he would attempt to put through conscription again in this Second World War.

It made no difference to Meighen and his supporters that conscription was almost completely unnecessary until 1944. It made no difference that there were few casualties to create any reinforcements shortage. It made no difference that the 1939-45 war was not fought in trenches like the Great War. Conscription to the Tories was not something rational. It was an article of faith in a creed of Empire. The only way to fight a war was through total conscription of manpower, the litany ran. To do anything less was to betray the Empire. The Liberal claims that Quebec would revolt were false. If the conscription act was well-handled, the French Canadians would fall into line and do as they were told. So ran the Conservative arguments.

But in fact Quebec would not have fallen into line. As in 1914-18, Quebec had no desire to fight a war for England—for so the war was seen in the province. "Listen," *Québecois* would say to English Canadians, "do you think Canada would be at war if England were not?" Who could answer affirmatively to this question? It was not enough to say that the Nazis were a menace to everyone, when the United States stayed out of the war until they were attacked by the Japanese. It was not enough to say that the war was a fight for democracy, when the Soviet Union was an ally of Britain. To Quebec the war was an English war, and if the English Canadians wanted to die for England that was their business. But they had no right to impose their perverse desires on the true North Americans, the true Canadians, the French Canadians.

Quebec's attitude was certainly not an idealistic one. It was narrow, selfish, isolationist. But it existed. So long as it was there, all that the government could do was try to "educate"

Quebec—and English Canada. Brooke Claxton, in 1942 a Liberal MP from Montreal and later a distinguished cabinet minister, hit the nail on the head when he wrote to a friend after Meighen's political demise in York South:

> Both parties have tried to deal with Quebec by building up bogies. We did it with conscription and Meighen. Now that Meighen has been stopped, I do not know how the province of Quebec is to be kept in line unless we can get another bogey or start telling the people in Quebec the plain truth. . . . We have to tell you people in Toronto and elsewhere that Canada is a nation of two races; that its only hope for union is in a single loyalty to Canada. And we have to tell the people of Quebec that they are members not only of Quebec but of all Canada and they can be no more isolated from the rest of Canada than Canada can be isolated from the world.[8]

If politicians cared for national unity they had to act in this fashion. Mackenzie King had used the "bogey" device before, but to his credit he tried to educate all Canada during the war years.

In fact, he was strikingly successful. In the Great War, probably no more than 35,000 French Canadians served in the armed forces. Between 1939 and 1945, however, between three and four times that number saw service. French Canadians in large numbers had come to realize that there was no security for Canada unless there was peace in the world.

There will never be another conscription crisis. The changed nature of warfare and the development of atomic weapons have ensured that. But today Canada faces new and equally dangerous threats to national unity, as extremists in Quebec and in English Canada try to split the country. The average citizen will probably have very little to say about the eventual resolution of this Canadian crisis, but he can do something if he remembers that sometimes compromise and delay, hesitation and caution are better than rigidly held positions. Expediency is a nasty word that is sometimes thrown at politicians when they hedge their bets or try to compromise. But sometimes it is better to practice expediency than to follow the wrong policy.

Notes

(THE ABBREVIATION P.A.C. IS USED TO DENOTE PUBLIC ARCHIVES OF CANADA.)

Chapter I

1. Arthur Lower, *Canadians in the Making* (Toronto: Longmans, 1958), pp. 395ff.
2. Hugh MacLennan, *Two Solitudes* (Toronto: Popular Library, n.d.), pp. 13/4.
3. Joseph Schull, *Laurier: The First Canadian* (Toronto: Macmillan, 1966).
4. P.A.C., J. S. Willison Papers, Byng to Willison, September 9, 1921.
5. P.A.C., Arthur Meighen Papers, T. Delany to Meighen, December 23, 1921.

Chapter II

1. P.A.C., Robert Borden Papers, Note by Loring Christie to Borden, n.d. (f. 148398).
2. P.A.C., J. W. Dafoe Papers, Grant Dexter to Dafoe citing a conversation with Norman Lambert, April 18, 1941.
3. Nancy Hooker (ed.), *The Moffat Papers* (Cambridge: The Harvard University Press, 1956), pp. 339/40.
4. *Toronto Daily Star,* March 28, 1939.
5. House of Commons *Debates,* March 30, 1939, p. 2426.
6. Queen's University, H. A. Bruce Papers, Bruce to Lord Beaverbrook, February 27, 1939.
7. P.A.C., Robert Manion Papers, Manion to Georges Héon, August 1, 1939.
8. C. P. Stacey, *Six Years of War* (Ottawa: Queen's Printer, 1955), pp. 40/1.
9. House of Commons *Debates,* September 7, 1939, p.1.
10. *Ibid.,* September 9, 1939, p. 73.
11. *Ibid.*
12. Janet A. Smith, *John Buchan, A Biography* (Boston: Little, Brown, 1965), p. 458.
13. P.A.C., R. B. Bennett Papers, Bennett to W. D. Herridge, September 18, 1939.
14. Queen's University, Norman Rogers Papers, "Conversation with Major General McNaughton . . .", October 4, 1939.
15. Michel Brunet, *Histoire du Canada par les textes,* vol. II, *1855-1960* (Montreal: Fides, 1963), pp. 128/29.
16. Norman Ward (ed.), *A Party Politician: The Memoirs of Chubby Power* (Toronto: Macmillan, 1966), p. 347.
17. Brunet, *op. cit.,* p. 130.
18. Ontario Department of Public Records and Archives, M. Hepburn Papers, Hepburn to W. M. Southam, December 1, 1939.

19. J. W. Pickersgill, *The Mackenzie King Record*, vol. I: *1939-44* (Toronto: University of Toronto Press, 1960), p. 62/3.
20. *Telegraph-Journal*, Saint John, January 27, 1940.
21. *Ottawa Journal*, March 20, 1942.
22. House of Commons *Debates*, May 21, 1940, p. 108.
23. *Statutes*, 4 Geo. VI, c. 13.

Chapter III

1. C. P. Stacey, *Six Years of War* (Ottawa: Queen's Printer, 1955), p. 121.
2. Meighen Papers, Memorandum, n.d.
3. P.A.C., Ernest Lapointe Papers.
4. E. Turcotte, "What Canada's War Effort Might Be," in A. R. M. Lower and J. F. Parkinson (eds.), *War and Reconstruction* (Toronto: Ryerson, 1942), p. 35.
5. "The Recruiting Problem...," in Lapointe Papers.
6. P.A.C., J. L. Ralston Papers, Memorandum, July 5, 1943.
7. Meighen Papers, Meighen to Bennett, July 24, 1941.
8. House of Commons *Debates*, May 12, 1941, p. 2729.
9. P.A.C., R. B. Hanson Papers, Hanson to H. C. Farthing, May 27, 1941.
10. Meighen Papers, Meighen to M. A. MacPherson, August 7, 1941.
11. *Evening Telegram*, Toronto, October 30, 1941.
12. Meighen Papers, Meighen to A. C. Casselman, October 31, 1941.
13. *Globe and Mail*, Toronto, November 4, 1941.
14. *Ibid.*
15. *Canadian Forum*, XXI (December, 1941), p. 260.
16. Meighen Papers, Meighen to H. Clark, November 14, 1941.
17. *Globe and Mail*, Toronto, November 13, 1941.
18. Pickersgill, *The Mackenzie King Record*, vol. I: *1939-44* (Toronto: University of Toronto Press, 1960), pp. 278/81.
19. *Toronto Daily Star*, January 10, 1942.
20. *Globe and Mail*, Toronto, January 12, 1942.
21. House of Commons *Debates*, January 22, 1942, p. 2.
22. *Globe and Mail*, Toronto, February 5, 1942.
23. Roger Graham, *Arthur Meighen*, vol. III, *No Surrender* (Toronto, Clarke, Irwin, 1965), pp. 126/27.
24. Pickersgill, *op. cit.*, p. 348.
25. House of Commons *Debates*, January 26, 1942, p. 26.
26. Hanson Papers, Hanson to H. A. Hanson, February 2, 1942.
27. Cited in Mason Wade, *The French Canadians, 1760-1945* (Toronto: Macmillan, 1956), p. 948.
28. André Laurendeau, *La crise de la conscription, 1942* (Montreal: Editions du Jour, 1962), p. 84.
29. *L'Aiglon*, 24 avril, 1942.
30. House of Commons *Debates*, June 10, 1942, p. 3236.

Chapter IV

1. *Ottawa Journal,* June 20, 1944.
2. Progressive Conservative party files, *War Policy, John Bracken on Record* (mimeographed statements by Bracken).
3. Rodney Adamson Papers, Diary, July 24, 1944.
4. Ralston Papers, L. Breen to Ralston, August 29, 1945.
5. *Globe and Mail,* Toronto, September 19, 1944.
6. Ralston Papers, Untitled remarks to Council, October 24, 1944.
7. R. MacGregor Dawson, *The Conscription Crisis of 1944* (Toronto: University of Toronto Press, 1961), p. 18.
8. E. L. M. Burns, *Manpower in the Canadian Army* (Toronto: Clarke, Irwin, 1956).
9. Dawson, *op. cit.,* p. 84.
10. Bruce Hutchison, *The Incredible Canadian* (Toronto: Longmans, Green, 1952), pp. 380ff.
11. Maurice Pope, *Soldiers and Politicians* (Toronto: University of Toronto Press, 1962), pp. 259-261n.
12. Dawson, *op. cit.,* p. 88.
13. Pope, *op. cit.,* pp. 259-261n.
14. Dawson, *op. cit.,* p. 84.
15. Dale Thomson, *Louis St. Laurent: Canadian* (Toronto: Macmillan, 1967), pp. 149/50.
16. Norman Ward (ed.), *A Party Politician: The Memoirs of Chubby Power* (Toronto: Macmillan, 1966), pp. 168/72.
17. House of Commons *Debates,* November 27, 1944, pp. 6617/18.
18. Meighen Papers, Meighen to G. O'Leary, November 23, 1944.
19. *Maclean's Magazine,* Toronto, January 1, 1945, p. 14.
20. Michel Brunet, *La Présence anglaise et les Canadiens* (Montreal: Beauchemin, 1958), pp. 250/51.

Chapter V

1. Progressive Conservative party press release, February 1, 1945.
2. Cited by J. L. Granatstein, *The Politics of Survival: The Conservative Party of Canada, 1939-45* (Toronto: University of Toronto Press, 1967), p. 184.
3. *Ottawa Journal,* May 16, 1945.
4. *Gazette,* Montreal, May 17, 1945.
5. *Maclean's Magazine,* Toronto, July 15, 1945, p. 15.
6. *La Presse,* Montreal, 4 juin, 1945.
7. *Ibid.,* 9 juin, 1945.
8. Dafoe Papers, Claxton to Dafoe, February 19, 1942, enclosing Claxton to J. M. Macdonnell, February 18, 1942.

Bibliographical Note

The Second World War is not a subject that has been seriously studied by Canadian historians. Few books deal with the years from 1939 to 1945 in anything more than a cursory fashion, and there are no great interpretations of the period. Undoubtedly this lack will be remedied in the future, but Canadian historians have been rather slow in the past to move into new areas.

Certainly there is no shortage of primary source materials already available. The Public Archives of Canada in Ottawa hold the letters of Arthur Meighen, R. B. Hanson, Robert Manion, Ernest Lapointe, W. L. Mackenzie King, and J. Layton Ralston. The Saskatchewan Provincial Archives have James Gardiner's papers, and Queen's University has the collections of T. A. Crerar and Chubby Power. The Roosevelt Library at Hyde Park, New York, contains substantial material relating to Canada, as do the papers of J. Pierrepont Moffat at Harvard University.

The essential published source for the Second World War is unquestionably J. W. Pickersgill's *The Mackenzie King Record*, Vol. 1: *1939-44* (Toronto: University of Toronto Press, 1960); Vol. 11: *1944-1945* (Toronto: University of Toronto Press, 1968). The student can also find sections of King's diary for the conscription crisis of 1944 in R. MacGregor Dawson, *The Conscription Crisis of 1944* (Toronto: University of Toronto Press, 1961). The interpretations in this volume should be used with care. The multi-volume official biography of Mackenzie King has not yet reached the Second World War years (and may never do so); as a result the best book on King as a war leader remains Bruce Hutchison's *The Incredible Canadian* (Toronto: Longmans, Green, 1952). Roger Graham's biography of *Arthur Meighen*, Vol. III: *No Surrender* (Toronto: Clarke, Irwin, 1965) treats the Conservative leader's role during the war in an uncritical fashion. *Louis St. Laurent: Canadian*

(Toronto: Macmillan, 1967) by Dale Thomson examines the career of King's Minister of Justice, and Chubby Power has produced excellent memoirs in Norman Ward (ed.), *A Party Politician: The Memoirs of Chubby Power* (Toronto: Macmillan, 1966).

Among other memoirs and biographies, the student should consult Neil McKenty, *Mitch Hepburn* (Toronto: McClelland and Stewart, 1967); General Maurice Pope, *Soldiers and Politicians* (Toronto: University of Toronto Press, 1962); Ramsay Cook, *The Politics of John W. Dafoe and the Free Press* (Toronto: University of Toronto Press, 1963); and Kenneth McNaught, *A Prophet in Politics: A Biography of J. S. Woodsworth* (Toronto: University of Toronto Press, 1959).

The Official History of the Canadian Army in the Second World War has been published in three volumes of which the first, *Six Years of War* (Ottawa: Queen's Printer, 1955), is the most valuable for politico-military content. General E. L. M. Burns' *Manpower in the Canadian Army* (Toronto: Clarke, Irwin, 1956) is an interesting little book. The history of the Conservative party during the war years has been examined by J. L. Granatstein in *The Politics of Survival: The Conservative Party of Canada, 1939-45* (Toronto: University of Toronto Press, 1967), and there is some useful material in James Eayrs' *The Art of the Possible* (Toronto: University of Toronto Press, 1961). The series *Canada in World Affairs*, published by the Canadian Institute of International Affairs, has three volumes on the war years, all of which discuss domestic politics. Finally the student could do worse than to examine volume two of Mason Wade's *The French Canadians, rev. ed.,* (Toronto: Macmillan, 1967), the only detailed treatment of Quebec response to the war.

Index

A

Adamson, Rodney: 55

B

"Baby Bonus": 53
Bennett, R. B.: 10, 15, 19
Bill 80: 47-8
Borden, Sir Robert: and Great War, 4-9; policy on conscription, 6-9
Bourassa, Henri: 4
Bracken, John: selected Conservative leader, 52-3; and Saskatchewan election 53-4; on conscription, 1944, 55; and Grey North by-election, 67-8; and conscription, 1945, 70-2
British Commonwealth Air Training Plan: 20
Bruce, Dr. Herbert: 33
Brunet, Michel: 66
Burns, General E. L. M.: 59
Byng of Vimy, Lord: 10

C

Canadian Army: troops to Europe, 1939, 20; uniform shortages, 24; strength, 1941, 30-1; problems with French Canadians, 31-3; role, 1941-1943, 49-51; at Hong Kong, 50-1; at Dieppe, 52; in France, 54; revolt of the generals, 61-3; in Northwest Europe, 66
Canadian Forum: 36
Cardin, P. J. A.: 14, 23, 47
Case, Garfield: 68
Church, T. L.: 18-9
Claxton, Brooke: 76
Committee for Total War: 39-40
Confederation: 2-3
Conscription: demands for, 1917, 5, 7; implementation, 1917, 8-9; in 1921 election, 10; in elections of 1925 and 1926, 10; pre-war party views on, 15-7; in Quebec election, 1939, 21-3; in 1940 election, 26-7; Conservative position on, 1940, 26-7; for home defence, 1940, 28-30; demand for in 1941, 33-4; in York South by-election, 38-41, 42; in 1944, 53-57; crisis of 1944, 56-65; NRMA troops sent overseas, 66; Power on, 64-5; and 1945 election, 70-3; for Pacific theatre, 70; effects of, 73-6
Conservative party: and election, 1911, 4; condition in 1939, 14-17; and weakness in Quebec, 15; organizational difficulties, 1940, 26; and conscription, 26-7, 33-5, 37, 42, 43, 53-5, 65-66; Ottawa meeting 1941, 35-7; dilemma re plebiscite, 40-42, 43; weak condition, 1942, 52-3; Port Hope Conference, 52-3; selects Bracken as leader, 52-3; changes name to Progressive Conservative, 52-3; reaction to McTague on conscription, 1944, 55; response to Grey North win, 68-9; and 1945 election, 70-3; and Quebec, 1945, 70-1; effect of conscription on, 74-5
Co-operative Commonwealth Federation: and war entry, 26; in York South by-election, 38, 41-2; increases strength, 52
Crerar, T. A.: 63

D

Dawson, R. M.: 61-3
Dieppe: 51
Douglas, T. C.: 53
Drew, George: 24, 26, 55; and Hong Kong Commission, 50-1; wins Ontario 73
Duff, Sir Lyman: 50-1
Duplessis, Maurice: 20-3, 70-1

1 2 3 4 5   75 74 73 72 71 70 69